S0-CDR-969

vi—The UNIX Screen Editor
Editor
A User's Guide

vi—The UNIX Screen Editor
A User's Guide

August Hansen

A Brady Book
Published by Prentice Hall Press
New York, NY 10023

Copyright © 1986 by Brady Communications Company, Inc.
All rights reserved
including the right of reproduction
in whole or in part in any form.

A Brady Book
Published by Prentice Hall Press
A Division of Simon & Schuster, Inc.
Gulf + Western Building
One Gulf + Western Plaza
New York, New York 10023

PRENTICE HALL PRESS is a trademark of Simon & Schuster, Inc.

Manufactured in the United States of America

1 2 3 4 5 6 7 8 9 10

Library of Congress Cataloging-in-Publication Data

Hansen, August.
  vi—the UNIX screen editor.

  "A Brady book."
  Includes index.
  1. Text editors (Computer programs)   2. vi (Computer
program)   3. UNIX (Computer operating system)   I. Title.
II. Title: vi—the U.N.I.X. screen editor.
QA76.76.T49H36   1986   652′.5   86-9519

ISBN 0-89303-928-4

Contents

About the Author

August (Augie) Hansen is a consultant in the allied fields of computers and communications. He holds a Bachelor's degree in electrical and electronics engineering and has 20 years of experience in areas of technology involving these fields.

The majority of his work experience has been on voice and data switching systems and general purpose timesharing computer systems while working at AT&T's Bell Laboratories and Information Systems units. He has been involved in the design and development of computer and communications products and in the preparation of user documentation for them.

He is a contributing editor to *PC Tech Journal* and writes frequently on UNIX and communications topics related to the IBM PC family of microcomputers.

Acknowledgments

The text and examples used in this book were prepared on several minicomputer and microcomputer versions of the UNIX system. The primary system was an AT&T PC6300 running SCO XENIX Version 3.0, Release 1.4. Editor versions ranging from 2.7 to 3.9 were used in different computer environments to test the examples.

I thank all of my former associates at Bell Laboratories and AT&T Information Systems for their support and for seven years of shared experiences using the UNIX system in its evolving forms in a production environment. I am particularly indebted to Carl Brandauer, Dave Custer, and Al Larson for their continuing inspiration and friendship, and to several anonymous reviewers for their insightful comments and suggestions.

I also wish to thank Deborah Corson for her hard work in pulling all the pieces together — a job that is unseen and unrecognized (unless it is done poorly). Thanks for doing it well.

And to my family, thanks for putting up with me during the struggle to meet my long-term objectives while trying to survive in the short term.

Preface

This book is a distillation of my experiences in learning to use the visual editor when it first became available as an unsupported program within Bell Laboratories and in teaching others to use vi for programming and document preparation activities in a hectic production environment. Although vi is not necessarily the best tool for the job, it is the most widely available visual editor for UNIX(tm), and with AT&T's inclusion of vi in System V, Release 2, it is now officially supported.

Augie Hansen
Denver, Colorado

Introduction

Before we begin using vi, we will review a bit of the history behind it to put its use in perspective. We will also establish some useful conventions to be used throughout this guide.

UNIX Editing

The vi (usually pronounced VEE-EYE, although some users call it VIE) editor suits the needs of many computer users. Historically, programmers and software engineers have formed one of the largest populations of vi users. Writers and editors and word-processing specialists working on documents of all descriptions are a comparably sized group. In more recent times, managers, administrators, and general office workers have swelled the ranks of vi users under the UNIX operating system.

Early text editors for creating and modifying files were line oriented. Such editors, typified by **ed** on UNIX systems, have what seem like rather spartan capabilities compared to vi, but they are usually very efficient in their use of computing resources, and they are typically more powerful than their outward appearances suggest. It is unfortunate that they are far less efficient when measured by their contribution to user productivity. This is the legacy of programs that were designed to work at least acceptably with slow, dumb printing terminals.

The Genesis of the vi editor

The **ex** editor, an extended and enhanced version of the UNIX line-by-line editor, **ed**, was developed at the University of California at Berkeley by William Joy. Among its many features is the visual mode, which can be accessed from within **ex** or directly from the UNIX command line by typing **vi**. Beginning with the release of

UNIX System V, AT&T began to support vi as part of the product, although it had been used within AT&T and Bell Laboratories for about five years before being officially adopted.

vi has become available on many UNIX systems and has steadily gained popularity over the years in spite of challenges from full-screen editors of more recent vintage. Other screen editors for UNIX include EMACS in several varieties (all based on the editor used for the MIT MACS project); se, an AT&T word-processing style editor that is available on some UNIX systems (it's no longer supported), and an alphabet soup list of editors (ned red, scred, abe, and so on) that have met with varying degrees of success. As the author of scred noted, it's very hard to come up with good names for editors because most of the obvious and fitting ones have been claimed.

In addition, PC/IX and IX/370, licensed versions of the UNIX system for the IBM PC and IBM 370, use INed, a full-screen editor with some interesting features and a combination of command and menu user interfaces. Emerging Technology Consultants produces the Professional Writers' Package, which includes its EDIX screen editor and WORDIX, a text processor, that has gained a strong following in the PC-DOS and MS-DOS operating system world. The product family is now sold by AT&T for use with its 3B line of UNIX systems and is sold on an OEM basis for other UNIX systems. Details about several of the most widely used of these editors can be found in Appendix D.

── *Variations in vi Implementations* ──

Numerous versions of vi are currently in use in the field. Where differences exist in the availability of commands or in the behavior of them, they will be noted in the text.

Because the vi program is provided in source form to suitably licensed customer sites, there may be other variations that were produced to fit vi onto a given machine or to provide modified or additional features. Your system administrator or a resident expert (often called a UNIX "guru") should be able to help you find out what local customs and features are in effect. Don't be timid about asking for help if you need it.

If you are the system administrator, read about and practice using vi as much as possible. With only a modest effort, you will begin to feel comfortable with vi. You'll find that helping others with their editing problems will force you to learn how to use it extensively and efficiently.

Host Environments

An advantage of learning to use vi is that the popularity and availability of UNIX is steadily increasing, and the vi editor is supported on the majority of UNIX installations. The effort you put into learning to use vi and related UNIX tools will most likely not be wasted when you move to a different UNIX system. Because vi is the screen editor officially supported by AT&T, it will likely be available on most UNIX systems you will use.

The numbers and types of microcomputers running UNIX have grown very quickly in the last few years. A representative sampling of microsystems includes the TRS-80 Model 16, most of the IBM PC family and compatible machines, intelligent work-stations from Sun Microsystems, a range of micro-based computers from AT&T, Hewlett-Packard, and even the Data General/One lap portable.

In addition, the range of minicomputers running UNIX is astounding. There are UNIX versions for the DEC PDP-11 and VAX-11 series, some Data General offerings, machines provided by Perkin-Elmer, Gould, Convergent Technology, and many other companies.

UNIX even runs on some mainframe computers, including an Amdahl (running UTS), the IBM 370 family running Maxi-UNIX and IX/370, and some of the Cray supercomputers.

Text and Keyboard Notation

Throughout this guide, we will use special typefaces and symbols to identify user input, system responses, and special characters. Certain control and special characters are understood by vi. A control character is a two-key combination requiring you to press and hold the key labeled CONTROL (or CTL, CTRL, CNTRL, and such), then press another key briefly before releasing both keys. The CONTROL key sequence will be designated by the symbol ^ followed immediately by a single character, displayed as an upper-case letter, although you may type the letter in either case. For example, the command to redraw the screen is ^L, which means to hold the CONTROL key and press the "L" key, then release both keys. Use of the SHIFT key or CAPSLOCK mode do not alter the meaning of the key sequence. This confusing way of symbolizing control characters is due to tradition born in the days of uppercase-only terminals.

Because the symbol for a control character usurps the caret symbol (^), in this book I will use ↑ to designate a caret and reserve the ^ symbol for use in indicating control characters only. This style is consistent with the prevailing practice in most UNIX documentation and its application programs.

Your input, that which you type on the keyboard, is shown in bold type. Components of your input that are variable, such as text or file names, are shown in bold italic type. For example, the command to edit a file will be shown as

vi *filename*<CR>

which has **vi** in bold meaning literal input and ***filename*** in bold italics indicating that you will supply the name of the file you want to edit.

Commands to the UNIX shell and some within vi are terminated with a carriage return. The return key is marked in various ways on different terminals and computers, so I will use the the sequence **<CR>** to symbolize whatever key on your keyboard produces the carriage return. Some terminal and computer keyboards have keys marked ENTER, LINEFEED, or a down arrow or left arrow. You may have to experiment a bit on your equipment to find out which key to use to terminate a command.

Similarly, I will use **<BS>** to symbolize a backspace key, which may be marked with the letters BS, BACK, or a left-facing arrow on some keyboards, and may not be present on others. The control-key sequence ^H produces the same internal code as a backspace key.

Editor responses will usually be shown as normal text except when the response would be displayed in some highlighting mode, which will be simulated in this text by bold printing with a continuous underline (**like this**).—

Describing an editor as complex as ex/vi poses a chicken and egg problem. It is impossible to avoid mentioning some topics in limited, specific uses before they are explained in detail in some later section. Forward references are used in such cases. Also, some detailed material is only alluded to in the main text. Details for those who care to read them have been placed in the appendices. After you have become proficient with the basics of editing, you should take a pass through some of the hidden detail to find things that may help you in your editing tasks.

With the formalities out of the way, it's time to begin editing with vi. The lessons assume that you have no specific knowledge of any editor. Each lesson identifies learning goals and has a set of helpful exercises at the end to test your knowledge of the material. To get the most benefit from the exercises, try to do them, preferably on a functioning system, to get a feel for how well you understand the lesson material.

Registered Trademarks

UNIX is a trademark of AT&T Bell Laboratories.

XENIX and Microsoft are trademarks of Microsoft Corporation.

DataGeneral/ONE is a trademark of Data General.

WordStar is a trademark of Micropro International Corporation.

Venix is a trademark of VenturCom, Inc.

IBM is a trademark of International Business Corporation.

EDIX, WORDIX, and Professional Writer's Package are trademarks of Emerging Technology Consultants, Inc.

DEC, VAX, and PDP are trademarks of Digital Equipment Corporation.

Multics is a trademark of Honeywell.

Limits of Liability and Disclaimer of Warranty

The author and publisher of this book have used their best efforts in preparing this book and the programs contained in it. These efforts include the development, research, and testing of the theories and programs to determine their effectiveness. The author and publisher make no warranty of any kind, expressed or implied, with regard to these programs or the documentation contained in this book. The author and publisher shall not be liable in any event for incidental or consequential damages in connection with, or arising out of, the furnishing, performance, or use of these programs.

Getting
Started

Goals

—Prepare your UNIX working environment for using the vi screen
editor

—Create some text in a file for editing

—View text using scrolling and paging commands

1.1 Initial Setup

Before using vi, you must do a few things. vi has to know what
type of terminal it is interacting with so it can correctly display
characters on the screen and interpret input from the keyboard.
Each terminal type has its own way of doing things. Programs like
vi automatically modify the way they work to accommodate a wide
range of terminals.

To find out whether a terminal type has been set in your UNIX
working environment, type **echo $TERM<CR>.** If no value has
been set, UNIX will reply with a new shell prompt on a new line. If
the TERM variable has been assigned a value, it will be displayed.
Be sure the value is an appropriate one for the terminal you are
using. See Appendix A for a list of terminal types recognized by
most computer systems running UNIX or a UNIX work-alike
operating system.

To tell the UNIX system what terminal you are using, if it doesn't already know, type the following commands from the command line ($ is the standard UNIX prompt from the Bourne shell). Assuming that your terminal is a DEC VT100, type

```
$ TERM=vt100
$ export TERM
```

to tell UNIX programs how to use the terminal correctly.

Of course, if you have something other than a VT100 terminal, you should use the appropriate name from the list in Appendix A. If the terminal is not listed there, use the UNIX **grep** program to search the terminal data base file, /etc/termcap, to see whether it's listed there. The procedure for doing the search is described in Appendix A.

The **export** command is required to let programs that you run, including vi, know about the value of TERM, which is a shell environment variable.

When using the C shell (**csh** is a Berkeley user interface program) on any UNIX system (% is the standard prompt), type

```
% setenv TERM vt100
```

to tell the system about your terminal. The **setenv** command combines the setting and exporting of the variable in one operation. Again, use the designation appropriate for your terminal.

These commands may instead be placed in your .profile shell start-up file (or in your .login under the Berkeley system) to be run automatically each time you log in. It is also possible to place the required information in a shell variable called EXINIT. Most versions of vi now support this feature. Appendix B describes how to set up your UNIX login environment for the use of vi.

1.2 *Creating Some Text*

To learn vi, or any other program of significance, you are going to have to practice. Trying to learn vi by only reading about it is like trying to become a ballet dancer or a world class skier without putting in the hours of practice needed to develop and sharpen your skills. Don't waste your time. Unless you have access to a UNIX system and a suitable terminal, spend your time on something more productive.

For the first few lessons, you will need some text in a file that you can edit without fear of losing something valuable. You will use vi to create a file called "US_Cons" that will demonstrate many of vi's features. After the file is prepared, a copy will be put in a safe place, and you can practice editing the file with reckless abandon.

Type the text just as you see it below; use the backspace key (**<BS>**) to correct mistakes as they occur. The UNIX system character-erase and line-kill characters can be used also. The values of these characters are usually set by UNIX system administrators so check with someone in authority if you don't know the values. On older UNIX installations they are usually # (character-erase) and @ (line-kill). XENIX and other versions of UNIX often preset these to ^H and ^U, respectively.

You will want the text to look exactly like it is shown below so that command actions and their on-screen results will match what is presented in the examples. For now, type the commands as they are shown without worrying about why. As you work your way through the following lessons, all of the commands will be explained in detail.

At the UNIX prompt ($ or % or whatever) type

vi US_Cons<CR>

and wait for vi to load and run.

When vi is ready, you will see a screen that is nearly blank except for a series of tildes (˜) running down the left side of the screen, a message on the bottom line of the screen that tells you the name of the file and some information about it, and a cursor at the upper left corner of the editing window.

```
                                                          SCREEN DATA
~
~
~
~
~
''US_Cons''  [New file]
```

The bottom line on the screen (excluding special status and function key label lines on some terminals) is usually called the vi status line because that is where messages from the editor are displayed. It is also called the ex command line because you can type most ex commands on this line as you will see shortly. Some early versions of vi produce the message "[No such file or directory]" instead of the "[New file]" message just shown. The meaning is the same a new file will be created if you input some text and save the editing buffer to disk.

On terminals running at high speed (1200 baud or faster), the editing window will usually occupy the entire screen except for the last line of the normal viewing area. Terminals running at slow speeds generally will display an editing window with fewer lines in it initially. You are free to change the window at any time by using the commands described in Lesson 3.

To create this new text, type **a,** followed by the text shown below, and end the activity with an **ESC** character. As you type in the text, end each line with a carriage return (shown as **<CR>**). Here is the text of the file, which is taken from the United State Constitution. The lines are all short so they can be printed easily on narrow pages and for other reasons that will become obvious later.

```
                                                    SCREEN DATA

We,<CR>
the people of the United States,<CR>
in order to form a more perfect Union,<CR>
establish justice,<CR>
insure domestic tranquility,<CR>
provide for the common defense,<CR>
promote the general welfare,<CR>
and secure the blessings of liberty to<CR>
ourselves and our posterity,<CR>
do ordain and establish this<CR>
Constitution for<CR>
the United States of America.<CR>
ESC
```

As you type each character, vi puts a copy of your input into a temporary working area called the editing buffer. To save this buffer in a file on disk, type **:w\<CR\>** and observe the message displayed by vi on the last line of the screen. It tells you the name of the file ("US__Cons") and its size in lines and characters. Now quit vi to do a few things before you return to look at the file and begin to learn about editing. Type the command **:q\<CR\>** to return to the UNIX shell.

Now make a backup copy of the file by typing **cp US__Cons US__Cons.bak\<CR\>**, which will create a copy of the file that you can use if the US__Cons file becomes lost or hopelessly scrambled.

1.3   *Starting vi*

Now you will use the file "US__Cons" as a vehicle for learning to edit using the UNIX screen editor. Because a copy of the file is in a safe place, there is no need to worry about doing something wrong. You can always recover the original text by copying it from the backup file.

As is true of many UNIX programs, vi has a wide range of options that may be specified when it is being started up. Options are signaled by a leading dash (-) and usually contain a letter or other symbol and possibly some additional information. Options change the behavior of vi in ways designed to meet special circumstances. I will defer a detailed description of options until later when they will make more sense in the context of editing a file. For now, simply call upon vi and name the file to begin editing that file. To edit the file you just created, type

vi US__Cons\<CR\>

and wait a moment while vi loads and copies the file into its editing buffer. This time, the screen will fill with some or all of the lines from the file, depending on the size of the window vi is using. Assuming a 23 line window, the screen should look like this.

```
                                                      SCREEN DATA
We,
the people of the United States,
in order to form a more perfect Union,
establish justice,
insure domestic tranquility,
provide for the common defense,
promote the general welfare,
and secure the blessings of liberty to
ourselves and our posterity,
do ordain and establish this
Constitution for
the United States of America.


~
~
~
~
~
~
~
~
~
~
''US_Cons'' 12 lines, 330 characters
```

The status line shows the name of the file and information about its size. Terminals with more or fewer than 24 display lines will, of course, have a different number of blank lines beyond the end of the buffer (indicated by the tildes).

For the commands that follow, we will want more text in the buffer—preferably 30 lines or more. So let's do the following to triple the amount of text available. Type **G** followed by **:r<CR>**. (If you type **g** instead of **G**, vi will complain—that is not a recognized command.) This sequence of commands adds a second copy of the file "US_Cons" to the end of the buffer. Repeat this to add another copy. Type **1G** (that's the number one, not a letter "el") to place the cursor on the first line of the editing buffer. Now there is a file in the editing buffer that is large enough (39 lines) to demonstrate some useful vi commands.

1.4   Viewing the Text

Once the file is ready to edit, you can look it over by scrolling or paging through it in the display window. The display window is the rectangular area on the screen in which you view all or a portion of the contents of the editing buffer. The display window size is the number of screen lines (or rows if you prefer) that will be affected by certain commands, such as those used for scrolling and paging.

Two types of editor commands are used in visual mode. The first type requires no termination character. You press a key and something happens. Commands of this type are typically used for cursor positioning and editing operations. The second type requires a colon (:) as the initial character and either a **<CR>** or **ESC** as a termination character. The commands of this type are, in fact, line-editing commands being executed from within the visual mode. Lesson 3 presents a detailed look at editor modes. For now, we will work within the visual mode and will use line-editing commands as they are needed.

Scrolling

The term scrolling comes from the ancient practice of perusing a rolled document, or scroll, by simultaneously unrolling one end and rolling the other to expose some portion of the material written or engraved on the document. Electronic documents are far easier to handle than ancient scrolls, but the concept of scrolling is common to both situations.

As new editing commands are introduced, both the functional name and the command sequence will be shown in a boxed display. The command sequence is contained in parentheses to set it off from the functional name. The parentheses are not part of the command.

Scroll down (*n*^D)

Scroll up (*n*^U)

---

vi recognizes ^D to mean scroll down the text of the file which moves the lines of text up on the terminal screen, thus exposing hidden lines, if any, at the bottom of the screen. When the end of the file is reached, vi stops scrolling and will reject further requests to scroll down and will either sound the terminal bell or flash the screen as a warning. Similarly, vi accepts ^U to mean scroll up in the file, which moves lines down on the screen to expose hidden lines at the top of the screen. Either of these commands may be preceded by a count, *n*, that tells vi how many lines to scroll. If a count is given, it is remembered and used for all subsequent scrolling actions until changed to another value by the same method. The default scroll value is approximately half the window size (usually 12 lines for a 23 line window).

Experiment with values on *n* in the range of one to 23: *n* must be an integer—one of the counting numbers. Notice where the cursor lands when you get near the beginning or end of the editing buffer. If there are fewer than *n* lines between the current position and the end of the file when a scroll down request is made, the cursor is moved to the last line of the file. Any further requests to scroll down are ignored and a warning is issued. Requests to scroll up are given similar treatment.

Reveal line(s) below the displayed window (*n*^E)

Reveal line(s) above the displayed window (*n*^Y)

These commands have no mnemonic value but are useful anyway. ^E attempts to scroll the screen so that another line, if one exists, from the editing buffer is revealed at the bottom of the display window. The cursor stays on the same line of the buffer if possible. The line currently at the top of the window moves out of view. Similarly, ^Y tries to reveal a new line at the top of the display window.

Both of these commands accept a preceding count, *n*, although the most likely value is the default of one. The count is forgotten (reverts to one) between invocations of these commands. Early versions of the editor do not offer these commands.

Paging

Paging produces a more abrupt change in the appearance of the screen than scrolling does. A page in this context is the display window size.

Page down (*n*^F)

Page up (*n*^B)

By typing ^F you tell vi to clear the screen and display a block of lines from a point further into the editing buffer than the current position. The number of lines to be displayed is equal to the window size. ^B moves the display window backward in the editing buffer by clearing the screen and displaying lines from a point closer to the beginning of the editing buffer.

An overlap of two lines is kept in most cases to provide continuity from one display to the next. The text display is redrawn from a point that is the window size minus two lines away from the current position. A count, *n*, receding the command tells vi to jump by that many pages, in which case a two-line overlap cannot be used. If there are not enough lines left in the direction you request paging, vi will signal an error (beep or screen flash) and not move the display window. You can move the cursor to the end of the buffer by using scroll commands or by using other commands described in the next lesson.

To see the effect of paging, first move to the beginning or end of the file and use the ^F or ^B commands to page through the buffer. Notice the overlapping lines that are used to retain some of the context from the previous page.

——————— *1.5 Saving Changes* ———————

Whether you are entering text for the first time or editing existing text, it is a good idea to save your editing buffer periodically to prevent loss of your work in the event of an unexpected error. Judge the interval by how much trouble it would be for you to repeat the work lost in such a situation. In Lesson 8 we'll learn about a way to have vi save the buffer automatically for you at an interval of your choosing.

Write buffer, continue editing (:w *filename*<CR>)

The file name is optional. When you start vi with a file name as an argument (as we did by typing **vi US__Cons<CR>**), vi remembers the name of the file. vi uses the currently remembered file name unless you specify a different file name. If *filename* differs from the current name, vi will create a file on disk called *filename*, filling it with a copy of the contents of the editing buffer. Therefore, to save this modified version of the "US__Cons" file for later use, we can give it the name "US__Cons3", which calls attention to the fact that it contains three copies of the same block of text. The command is **:w US__Cons3<CR>**.

If the file *filename* already exists and it has not been previously updated during the current editing session, vi will display a warning message because it tries to prevent accidental loss of an existing file. You can override this by appending an exclamation point to the command letter, as in **:w!** *filename*<CR>. This command will delete the named file's current contents and copy the buffer to that file. The remembered file name (called the "current" file) will not be changed by this command, but vi will retain *filename* as an "alternate" file, something we'll learn more about in Lesson 7.

In the formation of a "write" command, you must put one or more spaces or tabs between the command and the file name. The spaces or tabs form what is referred to as "whitespace", which is used to separate components of commands from one another. Commands that do not require whitespace are printed without any space between command characters.

1.6 *Quitting vi*

When you have finished viewing or editing the file, leave vi by using one of the following commands.

Quit (:**q<CR>**)

Write and quit vi (:**wq<CR>** or **ZZ**)

For our purposes, we would rather not change the contents of the original US__Cons file, so don't use the :**wq<CR>** or **ZZ** commands yet.

If you made no changes to the editing buffer since starting to use vi or since the last write command, a :**q<CR>** command will quit vi without writing the editing buffer contents back to the disk file.

You may use :**wq<CR>** or **ZZ** to save the editing buffer contents (write changes) to the remembered disk file and then quit vi. Both commands have the same effect as using a write command followed immediately by a quit command.

1.7 *Abandoning Changes*

In some situations, such as while learning to use vi, you may want to edit the buffer but not change the original file on disk. The safest technique, which we used earlier in this lesson, is to copy the file to a temporary file and edit the copy rather than the original file. But there are alternatives.

Quit without writing (:**q!<CR>**)

Reedit current file (:**e!<CR>**)

If you have already begun editing a file that you want to preserve in its original condition, abandon the changes and quit vi by typing **:q!<CR>**, which tells vi to make an immediate exit without writing the editing buffer out to disk. This is the correct choice for the work you are doing now, so try using this command to quit the current session. You should be left with the UNIX shell prompt.

Because vi remembers the name of the current file, the command **:e!<CR>** tells vi to ignore editing changes and read the remembered file's contents from disk into the editing buffer again. It's a convenient way to restart if you have modified the editing buffer beyond hope of a graceful recovery or if you just want to practice editing without altering the contents of the file.

─────────────── Exercises ───────────────

1. For your system and terminal, what is the correct set of commands to prepare for editing with vi?

2. What is the command to jump ahead three screen pages in the editing buffer? Back by two pages?

3. Write a single command that will scroll down in the editing buffer and set a new scroll value of eight lines.

4. What is the shorthand command that is equivalent to **:wq<CR>**?

5. How would you leave vi without updating the file on disk to match the modified editing buffer?

LESSON 2

Positioning the Cursor

Goals

—Move the cursor anywhere in the editing buffer

—Mark positions in the buffer and move to marked positions

—Search for characters and text strings

One of the most frequent actions performed during editing is positioning the cursor. Cursor positioning, for the purposes of the following descriptions, is divided into movements over characters and lines, textual words, and various text objects. There is considerable overlap among these categories. Each action is designed to get you from where you are to where you want to be in the editing buffer.

Cursor positioning is important because the cursor is a pointer into the editing buffer to the place where most of the work will be done. It is the focal point for the actions performed by your editing commands. The line that contains the cursor at any given moment is said to be the current line. The position occupied by the cursor is similarly referred to as the current position. A character that occupies the position marked by the cursor is said to be "at" or "under" the cursor.

—— 2.1 Character and Line Motions ——

The simplest and one of the most often used cursor motions is forward or backward one character or one line at a time. The commands for these motions may take a preceding count, *n*, which tells vi to multiply the effective range of the command by that many characters or lines. If a count is not specified, the default value of one is used.

Move left (*n*h or *n*^H or *n*<BS>)

If there are fewer than *n* characters to the left of the current position, any one of these commands moves the cursor to the first occupied position of the current line. It does not wrap back to the previous line. If the cursor is already at the beginning of the line, the cursor is not moved, and a warning beep or screen flash is issued.

Move down (*n*j or *n*^N or *n*+ or *n*<CR>)

These commands move the cursor down *n* lines, scrolling the display window if necessary. If there are fewer than *n* lines following the current line, the cursor does not move, and a warning is issued.

The **j** command tries to maintain the cursor in the same screen column in the destination line as in the starting line. The editor remembers the column position as you move up or down by one or more lines. If the number of occupied columns in the line the cursor lands on is less than the remembered value, the cursor is placed on the last position of the line. Further requests to move down a line will place the cursor at the remembered column position in lines that are long enough or the last position of lines that are not. The ^N form ("next" line) is synonymous with **j** and should be useable in all versions of vi, even some of the "prehistoric" versions of vi that did not use **j**.

The **<CR>** and **+** commands also move the cursor down a line; but, they place it at the beginning of the line regardless of the previous column position in a line. The beginning of the line is defined as the first column position occupied by a visible character. Leading whitespace (spaces and tabs) is ignored.

Move up (*n*k or *n*^P or *n*-)

These commands move the cursor up *n* lines. The display window will scroll if necessary to keep the cursor in view. If there are fewer than *n* lines preceding the current line, the command is ignored, and a warning is issued.

The **k** command attempts to maintain the current column position of the cursor (as described for the **j** command), but the – command moves the cursor to the beginning of the line. The ^P ("previous" line) is synonymous with **k** and should work in all versions of vi, whereas the **k** command is not implemented on some very early versions of vi.

Move right (*n*l or *n*<SPACE>)

If there are fewer than *n* characters to the right of the current position, these commands move the cursor to the last occupied position of the current line. The cursor does not move off the current line. If the cursor is already at the right-most occupied position of the line, it does not move and a warning is issued.

If the keyboard on your terminal has a special keypad with at least the four primary directional keys ("arrow" keys), you may use them to move the cursor. These would duplicate the controls just described. On some terminals (notably the hp2621) it is necessary for the arrow keys to be shifted for them to be acted upon by vi. Check the documentation for your terminal if you are not sure of the correct use of special keys.

2.2 *Word Motions*

Another often used set of commands moves the cursor in units called words. A word is a sequence of alphabetic and numeric characters that is separated from other character sequences by one or more blanks or tabs or by the invisible symbol that marks the separation between lines in the file (the ASCII newline). Some of the word-oriented commands also consider punctuation to be valid characters within words while others treat punctuation as word separators.

As with the character-motion commands, the word-motion commands may take a preceding count to multiply the effective range of the motion.

Word right (*n***w** or *n***W**)

The **w** command moves the cursor to the beginning of the word to the right of its current position, stopping at embedded punctuation marks. The **W** command considers punctuation to be part of a word. If the cursor is positioned anywhere in the last word on a line, this command wraps around to the next line to the beginning of the next word, if any.

If the cursor is within a word and a count, *n* is given, the current word is counted as the first of the *n* words.

End of word right (*n***e** or *n***E**)

These commands move to the end of the word past the current position in the file. The **e** command stops at embedded punctuation marks; the **E** command considers punctuation to be part of a word.

A count, *n*, may be given. If the cursor is anywhere within a word, that word is counted as the first of the *n* words. If the cursor is at the end of the last word on a line and more text follows, these commands will wrap around to the next line and leave the cursor on the end of the *n*th next word.

Back/Left (*n*b or *n*B)

These commands move the cursor back to the beginning of the word from the current position in the file. The **b** command stops at embedded punctuation marks; the **B** command considers punctuation to part of a word.

If the cursor is within a word, the word is counted as the first of the *n* words if a count is given. If the cursor is on the first character of the first word on a line, these commands wrap back to the beginning of the *n*th previous word on lines above the current line.

—— 2.3 *Moving to In-Line Objects* ——

v i provides several means of locating text objects in the editing buffer. Finding and moving to characters in the current line is accomplished with the following commands:

Find character to the right (*n*f*c*)

Find character to the left (*n*F*c*)

Repeat the find action (*n;* and *n,*)

The **f** and **F** commands move the cursor to the character *c* in the line if *c* exists. The **f** command looks for the character by searching to the right in the current line and the **F** command looks to the left. An error is signaled if the character is not found.

If *c* occurs more than once in the search direction, the cursor stops on the first occurrence, or on the *n*th occurrence if a count is given. A semicolon command (;) repeats the action of the find command in the direction of the original request, but it ignores any count given with the original request. Instead, it takes a preceding count of its own (assuming a value of one if none is given). The comma command (,) works the same way, but it reverses the direction of the search in the current line.

After finding the letter "e" in a line using **fe**, for example, you can find the second one to the right of the current position by typing **2;** or the next one to the left using the **,** command.

Move right to a character (***ntc***)

Move left to a character (***nTc***)

The **t** command searches to the right and moves the cursor to the character just to the left of **c** in the line if **c** exists. The **T** command searches to the left in the current line and moves the cursor to the character just to the right of **c** if it exists. An error is signaled if **c** is not found.

The **;** and **,** commands may be applied to these commands to repeat their effects, and both commands can be given a preceding count to multiply their effects. Thus, in the following line, the underlined characters are those found by successive uses of the forward repeat (**;**) command after a command to move to the letter "e" is given (**te**). The numbers on the second line show the sequence in which the individual find operations move the cursor to character positions. The cursor was originally on the 'a' at the beginning of the line.

SCREEN DATA

```
and secure the blessings of liberty to
     1   2   3   4              5
```

In each case, the cursor stops on the character just to the left of the designated letter. Although this may not seem to have significant application, you will see later that it is very useful when used with change and delete operators and when copying and moving blocks of text.

A few additional special characters specify frequently used objects—the beginning and end of a line and interior column positions, where "beginning" has two interpretations.

Move to beginning of line (↑ and **0**)

Move to end of line (**n$**)

↑ moves the cursor to the beginning of the current line and ignores spaces and tabs. The effect is to place the cursor in the first column that contains a visible character. It will not land on a whitespace character.

0 moves the cursor to the very first occupied position in the current line regardless of its content. Thus, if the line begins with a sequence of spaces, the cursor will land at the left-most position of the display window. If the first character is a tab, the cursor will rest on what looks like the eighth column (blank). This is the first *occupied* position in the line. Neither of these commands takes a count—they are constrained to the current line.

The **$** command moves the cursor to the end of the current line. **$** recognizes whitespace characters, so if the line contains space or tab characters after the last visible character, the cursor will appear to move past the end of line. When **$** is given a count, it moves the cursor to the *n*th end-of-line position past the current position in the buffer. The end of the current line is counted as the first of the *n* end-of-line positions.

Another command is used to seek any occupied column position in the current line.

Move to a column (**n|**)

The vertical bar and a preceding number, *n*, move the cursor to the *n*th column of the current line, if the line extends that far, or to the last occupied column on the line if it doesn't.

| by itself assumes column 0 and moves the cursor to the very first occupied position on the current line, regardless of its content. Thus, the cursor may land on a space or a tab character if it is the first character on the line. Without an *n* value, | is a synonym for **0**.

– *2.4 Moving to General Text Objects* –

To this point, you have learned how to move the cursor within a limited range of its current position. Commands that I will describe now position the cursor to any point in the editing buffer, either by directly moving it to a specified line or one relative to its current location, or by searching for a sequence of characters that you specify. Also, **v i** can return to previously marked positions anywhere in the buffer.

The general form of a command to move the cursor to a position in the editing buffer must contain at least a text object (symbolized by *OBJ*), and optionally a repetition count or line number reference (*n*).

Move to an object (*nOBJ*)

You have already encountered several text objects: **w** (and **W**) for the beginning of a word and **e** (and **E**) for the end of a word looking to the right, or in a "forward" direction; **b** (and **B**) for looking left or "backward" for the beginning of a word; line beginning (**0** and **↑**) and line end (**$**); and a column position (**|**).

Lines, sentences, paragraphs, sections, screen positions, and whole documents are generally called "higher level" text objects. The following commands move the cursor to such objects.

Go to a line (*n***G** or **:***n***<CR>**)

Sometimes you will want to move directly to a particular line in the file being edited. The **G** command causes the cursor to move to the beginning of the specified line, *n*, or to the last line in the buffer if no count is given. To move to the first line of the buffer, type **1G**. In each case, the cursor is placed at the beginning of the target line on the first visible character.

:$<CR> is the line-editing mode synonym for the visual mode **G** command. **$** is a shorthand notation for the last line in the editing buffer. If a number is used in place of the $ it is taken to be the literal line number.

Previous beginning of sentence (**n**())

Next beginning of sentence (**n**))

The separator between sentences varies with the position in a line. It is generally defined as a period (.), exclamation point (!), or question mark (?) followed by the newline character that terminates a line or by two spaces if the separation falls in the interior of a line. If you think of these commands as the viewing surface of an eyeball,) is looking to the right and down in the editing buffer and (is looking to the left and up.

For moves in either direction, the cursor will come to rest on the first character of a sentence, regardless of the direction of search. The search for a sentence separator is sometimes fooled by the presence of UNIX text formatter commands embedded in the text. This deception may result in the cursor being off by a line or two, which is not hard to recover from. vi has to assume that such codes separate sentences.

An optional count, **n**, causes vi to put the cursor on the first character of the **n**th sentence found from the current cursor position.

Previous beginning of paragraph (**n**{)

Next beginning of paragraph (**n**})

There are several ways to delimit a paragraph. The simplest is to place a blank line between paragraphs. In documents that contain UNIX text formatter commands, the character strings ".P " (a .P followed by a space), .bp, and other formatter commands may be recognized. The header and section formatter commands, like .H and .SH are also treated as paragraph markers because they usually implicitly begin a new paragraph.

To find out exactly what sequences **vi** is set to look for, type **:set para<CR>** and examine the "paragraphs" variable value that is displayed on the message line. The default is usually "paragraphs=IPLPPPPQP LIbp" or something close to this. The UNIX text formatters treat lines in a source file that have a dot in the first column as commands. The paragraph-variable value just shown instructs the editor to accept .IP, .LP, .PP, and other similar commands as paragraph delimiters. Therefore, the dot in such a command string would be a suitable resting place for the cursor after a **{** or **}** command to **vi**.

[NOTE: A detailed description of the **set** command will be presented in Lesson 8.]

Previous beginning of section (*n***[[**)

Next beginning of section (*n***]]**)

These commands are similar to those used to move by paragraphs except that the text object is a section. A section in a document is usually composed of many paragraphs. The use of a doubled command letter prevents unwanted movement over typically large distances in the editing buffer. It would be easy to type **[** or **]** by mistake.

The editor variable "sections" specifies what character sequences are interpreted by **vi** as delimiters of sections. Sections are treated analogously to paragraphs described above. You can use the command **:set sections<CR>** to determine what section formatting codes are known to the editor.

Find text string—forward search (**/***text***<CR>**)

Find text string—backward search (**?***text***<CR>**)

You can move the cursor to the beginning of a string of characters, *text*, using one of these two commands. Search forward in the buffer for a string by typing **/** followed by the search string, *text* and **<CR>**. If a match is found, you may continue the search in the same direction for the next instance of the same string by·typing **n** or in the reverse direction by typing **N**. Also, because the editor remembers the last search string, you can type **/<CR>** to repeat the search.

To search backward in the file, type **?** followed by the search string. If the editor variable **wrapscan** is set (Lesson 8), the editor will search around the end of the editing buffer by treating it as an unbroken loop.

There are many options available for searches of this type. Full "regular expression" syntax may be used in specifying search strings. A regular expression may contain ambiguous characters that have special meaning to v i (and other UNIX programs including the shell) in addition to normal text. For now, only two are noted: ↑ and $. These are used to force pattern matches to occur only at the beginning (↑) and end ($) of a line. This behavior is called anchoring. Regular expressions are described in Appendix D.

To search for the word "the" that occurs at the beginning of a line and nowhere else, type **/↑the<CR>**. Recall that ↑ represents the caret, usually a shifted "6" on the terminal keyboard, and it anchors searches to the beginning of a line and ignores spaces and tabs.

Conversely, **$** anchors searches at the end of a line, so **/thingamajig$<CR>** would find a match only if "thingamajig" occurs at the end of a line. Putting the two together in a search can help you move quickly to the next blank line: **/↑$<CR>** looks for a line that contains no text, not even spaces or tabs.

Two special metacharacters may be used to force a match at the beginning or ending of a word. **\<** (match the beginning segment of a word) and **\>** (match the ending segment of a word) are not part of the specification of regular expressions contained in the **UNIX User's Manual** in regexp(5) and ed(1). To find the word "the" and not "their", "there", and "together", you can type **/\<the\><CR>**, which constrains the search pattern to match the string "the" only where it is an entire word. (Note: The < and > surrounding CR are part of our symbol for the RETURN key, not separate characters to be typed in the search string.)

Similarly, you can match strings that begin or end with a sequence of characters by using only one of the special matching metacharacters. Thus, **/key\><CR>** matches the "key" in "monkey" but not in "keyboard."

— 2.5 *Moving to Window Positions* —

Relative and absolute positions within the display window make up another set of useful objects.

Top of window (*n***H**)

Middle of window (**M**)

Bottom of window (*n***L**)

These commands move the cursor to locations within the current viewing window. **H** moves the cursor to the "home" position, which is the upper left corner of the active viewing area. **M** places the cursor at approximately the middle line of the viewing area, and **L** moves the cursor to the lower left. Both **H** and **L** can take a preceding count. *n***H** puts the cursor at the beginning of the *n*th line from the top of the viewing area. Similarly, *n***L** puts it on the *n*th line from the bottom of the viewing area. Unreasonable requests (*n* larger than the window size, for example) are handled gracefully. The screen is scrolled if you type **30L** when there are only 20 lines in the window but only if there are enough lines in the editing buffer to satisfy the request.

2.6 *Marking and Returning to Buffer* Positions

It is also possible to put a mark in the editing buffer to make it easy to return to a spot visited earlier. The technique is called "marking and returning" and parallels the use of physical bookmarks.

Mark current position (**m***c*)

Move to marked line (**'***c*)

Move to mark (**`***c*)

To place a mark in the buffer, type **m** followed immediately by a lowercase letter. For example, **ma** places an invisible mark identified as **a** in the buffer at the current position. You may mark up to 26 positions in the buffer, one for each letter of the alphabet. The mark letters do not show in the displayed text, but are remembered by v i. A mark will be retained in the buffer until you either delete the text which contains the mark, in which case the mark is forgotten, or until you reuse the mark letter.

To return to a previously marked position in the file, type ` (back quote) followed by the marking letter, **a** for our example. This will move the cursor to the exact position you marked earlier. Typing a normal single quote and the mark letter, **'a**, moves the cursor to the beginning of the line containing the mark rather than to the exact position of the mark within the line.

As an extension of the mark and return capability, v i allows you to return to the previous context even though you did not explicitly mark it yourself. v i automatically places an invisible unnamed mark in the editing buffer where the cursor is positioned before moving it to a new position. v i records a mark for motions caused by such actions as a string search or positioning to an absolute line number. It does not mark the cursor position for local moves like simple cursor movements using arrow keys.

You may return to the immediately previous context by typing " (two single quotes—moves to the beginning of the line) or `` (two back quotes—exact position). These commands are handy when used with the search commands to find some needed text to move or copy to the current position in the file.

————————————————— Exercises —————————————————

1. Start **vi** and edit the "US__Cons" file. Practice moving the cursor one word at a time in both directions by using **w**, **W**, **b**, and **B** commands. Then use the **e** and **E** commands to seek the end of a word. Notice the difference in behavior of the commands that use punctuation to delimit words versus those that don't.

2. What is the briefest command you can type to move the cursor to the end of the editing buffer? To the beginning, if you are not already there?

3. In the following line of text, what is the optimum command sequence to find the third occurrence of the letter "t" after the cursor position? (The underline marks the current cursor position.)

SCREEN DATA

That's all there is to it, my friend.

---

4. With the file "US__Cons" in **vi**'s editing buffer and the cursor at the beginning of the first line, type a command to find the first occurrence of the word "States". What command does this? How would you find the next occurrence?

5. Move to the end of the editing buffer and type the command to search backward for the word "Union" and then move to the end of that line. What commands did you use?

Editor Modes and Window Control

Goals

—Understand the various components of the editor and their relationships

—Insert and append text in the editing buffer

—Use actions, counts, objects, and buffers to form a wide range of vi editing commands

—Control the editing window's initial appearance and operating characteristics

3.1 Editor Structure

The names vi and ex both refer to the same program, but when called ex, the program assumes the characteristics of a line editor, and when called vi, it takes on its *alter ego* personality[1] and operates in the full-screen visual mode.

---

[1]This schizophrenic behavior is not the exclusive domain of the ex/vi editor. The UNIX System III and V cp, ln, and mv commands are the same program called by different names to do different but related tasks. Other UNIX commands employ this same useful tactic of being linked to one or more aliases. UNIX programs can determine what name was used to call them and can alter their behavior accordingly.

ex is an extended version of the standard UNIX editor, ed. ed is exclusively a line-oriented editor, which means it operates on one line at a time, and it includes a range of powerful and flexible global editing features. Operations that affect more than one line (a global search and replace, for example) are actually executed as a sequence of one-line operations.

Two special modes of operation of the ex editor that are not found in the original ed editor are the visual (vi) and open modes, each having a subordinate text insertion mode. Although the focus of this book is on display editing, it will also cover the other ex modes to provide you with a working knowledge of the entire editor. Most users will be able to do the bulk of their work in visual mode with only temporary escapes to run ex commands.

Figure 3-1 shows the relationships among the various parts of the editor and highlights the modes used in screen-editing.

The figure depicts the modes of editor operation as bubbles connected by lines. Each line represents the action that causes the mode to change. The label next to each line is the command letter or name that you type to produce the action.

From the UNIX shell, typing **vi<CR>** starts up the editor in the visual editing mode. If instead you type **ex<CR>**, the editor starts in the line-oriented mode. It is easy to switch between the two modes. To go from visual mode to line mode, type **Q**. ex uses a : prompt to indicate that it is waiting for your command. To switch to visual mode from ex, at the prompt type **vi<CR>**.

Open mode can only be reached from the ex command line. It is a special form of the visual mode that operates like a single-line editor, allowing use of most vi commands even on hard-copy printing terminals. It is also useful on very slow dial-up connections and with some low-IQ video terminals that might as well be printing terminals. At the ex prompt, type **open<CR>** to enter open mode. To return to ex mode from open mode, type **Q**.

The use of ex and open editing modes is described in detail in Lesson 10. Nearly everything you learn about visual editing will be applicable in slightly modified form to open-mode editing.

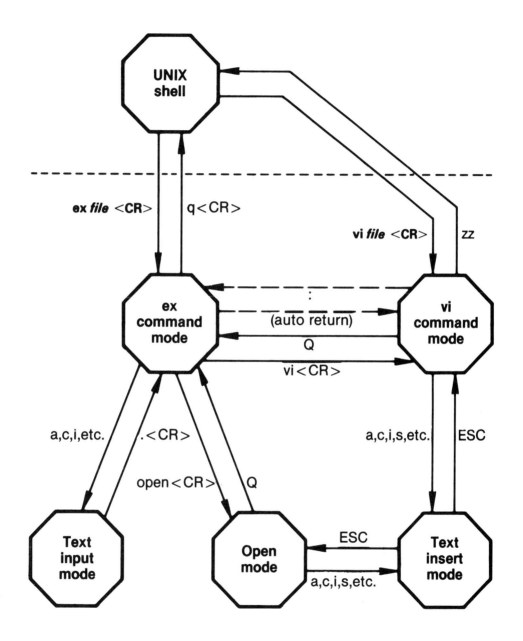

Figure 3-1. Modes of the ex/vi editor.

——————— *3.2 vi Command Mode* ———————

Thus far, we have used only the **vi** command mode and only for positioning the cursor and moving the display window in the editing buffer. This is the default **vi** mode. The visual command mode offers a very general and flexible set of commands which we will explore in great detail in this and later lessons.

As Figure 3-1 shows, many of the visual mode commands cause the editor to change to other modes. In editing a file, you will typically call upon two other modes from visual mode: the text insertion mode and the **ex** command mode.

——————— *3.3 vi Text Insert Mode* ———————

The visual text insertion mode, "insert mode" for short, is entered from the visual command mode by typing a text entry command, such as **i**, **a**, **o**, their variants, and a few other commands that you will learn about in the next lesson. By typing an **ESC** character you terminate the insert and return to visual command mode. Some recent versions (3.9) of the editor display a message at the right end of the status line to indicate when the editor is in the insert mode. For true insert mode, the message is "INSERT MODE", for continuous overtype mode it is "REPLACE", and for single-character replacement it is "REPLACE 1 CHAR" (more on these later).

Any amount of text may be typed during insert mode. The following command sequences cause **vi** to go into the insert mode, accept your input, and return to the command mode when you indicate that you have finished typing your input.

Append text after the cursor (*natext***ESC**)

Append text to end of line (*nAtext***ESC**)

The append command, **a**, places new text after the current character position, pushing existing text after the cursor position further to the right. The sequence

a School's really great.ESC

appends the sentence " School's really great." following the position marked by the cursor. Note the two leading spaces in the insert string following the **a** command. **vi** requires that a period be followed by two spaces to mark a sentence boundary. The UNIX text formatters automatically insert two spaces between sentences. If you put only one space after a period, **vi** will not consider it to be a sentence boundary.

Before:

```
                                                    SCREEN DATA

Hi Mom_.  Please send money!
```

After:

```
                                                    SCREEN DATA

Hi Mom.  School's really great_.  Please send money!
```

When the **A** command is typed, the append command places new text after the last character of the current line. Therefore, **A addendumESC** would tack a space and "addendum" onto the end of the current line regardless of the position of the cursor in the line. The **A** command is equivalent to a $ to place the cursor at the end of the line, followed by an **a** command to append after the cursor.

Either of the append commands can take an optional count to multiply the effect. A suitable example around the Christmas holiday might be typing **3A Ho!ESC** to append Santa's oft heard triplet to the end of the current line of text.

Before:

```
                                                    SCREEN DATA

...and to all a good night.
```

(The cursor position is irrelevant.)

After:

```
                                                      SCREEN DATA
  ...and to all a good night._Ho! Ho! Ho!
```

Insert text before the cursor (*itext***ESC**)

Insert text at beginning of line (**I***text***ESC**)

The insert command, **i**, puts new characters in the editing buffer to the left of the cursor as you type them and moves existing text to the right as each new character is inserted. Typing the insert command, **i**, followed by **fancy ESC** places the word "fancy " (note the trailing space that delimits a word) in the current line at the cursor position.

Before:

```
                                                      SCREEN DATA
  I like your new car!
```

After:

```
                                                      SCREEN DATA
  I like your fancy__new car!
```

When the insert operation is completed, the cursor rests on the space between words because that is the last character of the inserted text.

The **I** command places the inserted text at the beginning of the current line. The cursor may be anywhere in the line. **I** is equivalent to ↑ (move the cursor to the beginning of a line) followed by **i** (insert text). The beginning of the line is defined as the position of the first nonwhitespace character, so **INew textESC** places "New text" after any leading blanks or tabs but before any displayed characters on the line. Existing text is pushed to the right to accommodate the inserted text.

Other commands that cause insert mode to be entered (change, substitute, replace) are described in the next lesson.

Open a line for input (**o** or **O**)

The commands **o** and **O** open a line for input below and above the current line, respectively. It doesn't matter where the cursor is located in the current line when the open-for-input command is given. The effect is to spread apart the editing buffer at the designated location, switch to insert mode and accept input, and terminate the input upon receipt of an **ESC** character. The same effect could be achieved by moving to the end of a line and appending text at that point; but, the open commands are quicker and easier. Typing **o** has the following effect on the editing buffer.

Before:

```
                                          SCREEN DATA

alpha
bravo
delta
echo

```

After:

```
                                          SCREEN DATA

alpha
bravo

___
delta
echo

```

As with any insert operation, the inserted text may be any size from no characters (leaves a blank line) to the maximum allowed by available storage. The editor limitations usually exceed the storage capacity of the host system, especially in microcomputer environments, so they generally are of no concern. Recent versions of the editor can manage 250,000 lines of up to 1024 characters each.

Don't confuse the open-a-line-for-insert commands with the open mode of the editor. The former commands are editing commands while the latter command is an editor mode. In fact, you can use the **o** and **O** commands while editing in open mode just as you can in visual mode.

3.4   ex Modes

From the **vi** command mode, you may call upon most of the line-oriented commands. As we've seen, typing a colon while in the visual command mode temporarily accesses the line editor's command mode, moves the cursor to the status line, displays a prompt (":"), and awaits your request. Unlike the **Q** command, which makes a permanent switch to line-editing mode, the : forces a temporary mode change for the duration of one command.

Nearly all **ex** commands may be used at this point. The very powerful global commands and other line-editing features of the line editor are, thus, available without the need to leave visual mode. Some tasks lend themselves to the use of line-oriented commands, while many are aided by having the real-time visual feedback afforded by visual mode. Choose the editing mode that best suits the task at hand.

We will look closely at **ex** commands in Lesson 10. For now, just the "write file" and "quit editing" commands that you have already learned will be used.

3.5   General vi Command Syntax

The general command syntax for **vi** commands is

`[named_buffer][operator][number]object`

where surrounding square brackets mean the enclosed item is optional and the components are the following:

— named__buffer: a temporary text storage area in memory

— action: a verb that tells v i what to do

— number: a whole decimal value that specifies either the extent of the action or a line address

— object: a noun telling v i what object to act upon

Many objects are known to v i, most of which you have already seen, that fall into two broad categories. Here is a summary:

— Text objects: character, word, sentence, paragraph, section, character string

— Position: line, position in current line (beginning, end, column), screen position (top, middle, bottom)

A position is considered to be an object because it may be used to mark the beginning or end of some portion of the buffer that defines a region of text on which an operator acts.

Some commands combine the action and the object into a single entity. We have already seen how the $ signifies the end of the current line and how, as a command, $ moves the cursor to the end of the line. A right parenthesis signifies the beginning of a sentence to the right of the current position. Therefore, as a command,) moves the cursor to the beginning of the next sentence.

These and other text objects that can be used as action-object commands are summarized in Table 3-1.

— *3.6 General ex Command Syntax* —

Line editing and file system commands of the ex editor are available to you from v i mode. The primary ones we have already used are :w<CR> and :q<CR>. There are many more ex commands available to you; the global editing commands are of greatest interest.

Table 3-1. Text Objects Known to vi

Object	Description
↑ (caret)	First non-whitespace position in current line. (‗, an underscore, is a synonym for the caret.)
0 (zero)	First position in current line, even if it's a space or a tab.
number	A non-zero number is taken to be a line number in the buffer by 'goto' commands.
$	End of the current line (last occupied position) even if it's whitespace.
|	An occupied column position in the current line. With a count, the cursor goes to that position; without a count, | is a synonym for 0.
' (quote)	A mark at the beginning of the line that the regards as the previous 'current' line.
` (backquote)	A mark at the last cursor position in the line that the editor regards as the previous 'current' line.
%	Balancing parenthesis, bracket, or brace for the one at the cursor.
) and (	Beginning of sentence in forward and reverse directions from cursor.
} and {	Beginning of paragraph in forward and reverse directions from cursor.
]] and [[	Beginning of section in forward and reverse directions from cursor.
H, L, and M	The top-left (home), lower-left, and middle editing window positions.
b and B	Beginning of a word ahead of cursor position (B considers punctuation to be part of a word).
e and E	End of a word after cursor position (E considers punctuation to be part of a word).
w and W	Beginning of a word after cursor position (W considers punctuation to be part of a word).
c or *string*	Any text character or string of characters is an object for find, to, and search commands.

Run an ex command (:)

When you type the :, vi responds by echoing a colon prompt on the status line, where it then awaits your request. The general syntax of line-editing commands is

: *[address]* *[command]* *[!]* *[parameters]* *[flags]* <CR>

All components are optional except for the terminating <CR>.[2] The [and] characters are never typed—they just indicate the optional nature of the component enclosed within. In Lessons 6 and 7 you will learn to use many of the file handling commands accessible from line-editing mode.

———— *3.7 Window Control* ————

The transmission speed of the communications link to UNIX and the intelligence and speed of your terminal strongly influence the apparent responsiveness of vi to your commands. You can control certain critical factors that will improve responsiveness in many situations. Terminals that have insert and delete features built in can do many operations a lot faster than terminals that don't. Terminals that respond quickly to commands don't require the time wasters (called padding) that the editor uses to keep from getting ahead of slower terminals. Terminals that are slow and that lack built-in editing features are disparagingly called "dumb" terminals.

Set window—cursor at top (*nzm*<CR>)

Set window—cursor in middle (*nzm.*)

Set window—cursor at bottom (*nzm-*)

[2]An **ESC** may be used here in place of the <CR>, but in the permanent line-editing mode this is not the case. If you will be switching back and forth between visual and line modes, always use <CR> to avoid sending commands that ex doesn't understand.

Use these commands to adjust the size of the display window and to position the cursor where you want it. A small window doesn't show as much at one time as a full window, but as few as four or five lines is usually enough to provide the needed editing context. Small window sizes are of significant benefit when a terminal is being used over a slow-speed line. If you need a helpful mnemonic, think of the **z** command as "zeroing in" on a portion of the editing buffer.

Several functions are being performed by these commands, and they can be a bit confusing at first. Let's divide the problem into more manageable pieces. The minimum command is a **z** followed by one of the positioning command characters, **<CR>**, ., or -. The command **z<CR>** redraws the display at the current window size and places what is now the current line at the top of the redrawn window with the cursor at the beginning of the line.

Using **z** with the dot (.) and minus (-) terminating characters produces a screen at the current window size, but the current line, and, therefore, the cursor are placed in the middle and at the bottom of the window, respectively. Here "middle" is loosely interpreted by **vi** to mean somewhere other than the top and bottom lines of the window, but generally within a line or two of the middle, unless the window is less than three lines tall.

The preceding number *n* is an optional line address. It specifies what line to adjust the window around instead of the current line. If, for example, the command **7z.** is given, **vi** will redraw the window with line seven roughly in the middle and the cursor at the beginning of that line, which becomes the new current line.

The count *m* is also optional. It sets the window size in lines. The command **z5<CR>** redraws the display with a five-line window and what is now the current line at the top. The value specified by **m** is retained by **vi** as the current window size until it is changed by the **z** command or one of the other commands that has a side effect of altering window size. Attempts to set a window size larger than the terminal can support will cause **vi** to use the maximum window size that is set in /etc/termcap for the terminal.

All of these components can be used in a single command to change the current line, adjust the size of the current window, and place the current line at the top, middle, or bottom of the redrawn window. For example, the command **30z8-** makes line 30 current (cursor at the beginning of the line), sets the window to eight lines, and places the current line at the bottom of the window.

Search and "zero" window at top (*/text/zm*<CR>)

Search and "zero" window in middle (*/text/zm.*<CR>)

Search and "zero" window at bottom (*/text/zm-*<CR>)

Using the **z** command in tandem with a search command produces a useful effect. A match to the search provides the line address that precedes the **z** command. If a search is likely to have many matches, it is helpful to reduce the size of the window to minimize the time required to refresh the screen. This statement is especially true on low-speed connections and with dumb terminals. Typing a search in the form */text/zm.*<CR> or *?text?zm.*<CR> will place the line containing a matching string, if any, in the middle of an *m* line window. If there is no match, the window size and current line values are unchanged.

--- Exercises ---

1. Name the major operating modes of the **ex**/**vi** editor. Which of these modes are the most frequently used for visual editing? Which mode is used when reading and writing disk files?

2. Where will the text of the following insert command be placed in the line shown on the simulated display? **IPlease close the door on your way out. ESC** is the command. (**I** is the insert command and the **ESC** terminates the insert operation.) The underline marks the current cursor position. Where will the cursor be located after the insertion?

SCREEN DATA

Goodbye.

3. What command would you use to place the current line at the top of a five-line window? To place the twentieth line of a 50-line file at the bottom of a ten-line window?

4. List the commands needed to find a string of text in the editing buffer and insert a lone space ahead of it.

5. What is a whitespace character? What is the significance of a whitespace character at the beginning of a line to commands like **0** and **↑**?

6. Type the minimum number of commands needed to append the string "EOS" (not including the quotes) at the end of the current line? Now show how to append the same string at the end of the next line without retyping the string? At the end of the first line on the screen?

LESSON

4

Modifying Text

Goals

—Repeat the effect of a command

—Use delete, change, substitute, and replace commands

—Use simple command combinations to move or copy text

4.1 Repeating Commands

If you run a visual mode command that changes the editing buffer in some way and want to repeat it, you can instruct v i to do so by typing a dot (.). This comes in handy when you search for something with the / or ? commands, perform some command on the found object, and want to selectively repeat the command sequence on other matching objects. An **n** or **N** command finds the next match, if there is one, and a dot (.) command repeats the action performed on the previous matching object.

A count given to the repeat command is passed to the command being repeated. Therefore, if you delete a line by typing **dd**, you can then type 5. to delete five more lines. Commands that don't accept counts silently ignore any count given to the repeat command.

You will use v i as much for the manipulation of existing text as for the creation of new text. Even when new text is being created,

41

it is often necessary to rearrange it, modify it, and correct errors.
v i offers a rich set of commands for modifying text.

—————— *4.2 Deleting Text* ——————

Two delete commands are available in visual mode. The first is a
single-character delete, and the second is a general text deletion
capability that offers considerable flexibility.

Single-Character Delete (*n*x or *n*X)

The simplest deletion is the single-character delete, **x**, which
takes an optional number prefix to multiply its effect. Without a
prefix, **x** deletes the character at the cursor position and closes up
the resulting space by shifting the remainder of the line one
character to the left. **X** deletes the character just to the left of the
cursor and similarly closes up the line.

To delete more than one character, use the optional prefix
number, as in **4x** to delete four characters beginning at the cursor
position. **10X** deletes the 10 characters immediately to the left of
the cursor position.

The effect can be seen below. Typing **13x** tells v i to delete the
character at the cursor position and the **12** immediately to its right
and to close up the hole this creates in the line.

Before:

SCREEN DATA

Out ⌴ damned spot!

After:

SCREEN DATA

Out !

If the cursor is at the beginning of the line, any **X** command will be ignored and an error will be signaled. If there are between one and *n* characters between the beginning of the line and the cursor, an **X** command will delete the characters in all positions up to but not including the cursor position and shift the remainder of the line left to close up the vacated space.

The single-character delete, even when multiplied by a count, is not very flexible, so additional deletion commands are provided. You may delete one or more text objects of any description by using the following commands.

Delete Text (**d*n*OBJ** or **n*d*OBJ**)

This form of the command deletes *n* objects. For example, the command **d3w** deletes three words (taking punctuation into account) and closes up the line. (The command may be typed as **3dw** also. If two numbers are given, as in **3d3w**, the effect is literally multiplied, so an equivalent command is **9dw**.)

The command **dw** deletes from the cursor position to the end of the word containing the cursor plus the space separating the current word from the next word, if any. Unless given special instructions, vi also treats a punctuation mark as a separator, but does not delete it. To force vi to treat punctuation marks and other special characters as part of a word, use the **d*n*W** form of the command. Here is a C language example to demonstrate the difference in behavior of these two forms of the delete-word command.

Before using **dw** or **dW**:

SCREEN DATA

```
printf(''%s\n'', progname);
```

After using **dw**:

```
                                              SCREEN DATA
 ⌊''%s\n'', progname);
```

After using **dW**:

```
                                              SCREEN DATA
 progname);
```

The **dw** form stops deleting just left of the punctuation mark, but the **dW** form deletes all characters in the string up to and including the trailing space.

Returning to the example used to demonstrate the use of **x, d3w** is an easier way to get the same result as **13x** because you don't have to count characters, only words. Three "words" must be deleted because the cursor is on a punctuation mark. **vi** counts the comma and the following space as word one, and ends word three to the left of the exclamation point.

Before:

```
                                              SCREEN DATA
 Outͺ damned spot!
```

After **d3w**:

```
                                              SCREEN DATA
 Out !
```

Doubling the **d** to create the command **dd** instructs **vi** to operate on whole lines as objects.

```
 Delete Line (nnd)
```

To delete whole lines, type **ndd**. Thus, **6dd** tells vi to delete six lines including the line containing the cursor. After the deletion, the text will be closed up, and the cursor will be placed at the start of the line following the deleted lines.

Delete to End of Line (**nd$** or **D**)

The command **d$** tells the editor to delete all characters in the current line from the one at the cursor to the end of the line. **D** is a synonym for **d$**.

The first form of the command takes an optional count **n** either before or after the **d** (the default is one as usual). All characters from and including the one at the cursor to the **n**th end of line past the cursor are deleted and the cursor is placed at the end of the truncated line.

The **D** form of the command takes no preceding count and will ignore one if it is given. The cursor is placed at the end of the resulting line. To rid the following line of its sarcastic conclusion, move the cursor to the end of the first sentence by a convenient method and type **D**.

Before:

SCREEN DATA

Eat, drink, and be merry!__ Suffer in the morning.

After:

SCREEN DATA

Eat, drink, and be merry!_

The person who edited this chooses not to worry about tomorrow morning until it gets here.

The object for deletion specified by **OBJ** can also be selected with find (**fc**), move to (**tc**), search (**/text<CR>**), and other commands that define a range of text to delete to the right or left of the cursor position. Using our text example, first move the cursor to the U in United States. Then type the command **d/Union<CR>**.

Before:

```
                                                    SCREEN DATA
We,
the people of the United States,
in order to form a more perfect Union,
establish justice,
insure domestic tranquility,
...
```

After **d/Union<CR>**:

```
                                                    SCREEN DATA
We,
the people of the Union,
establish justice,
insure domestic tranquility,
...
```

Try some of the other alternatives by using find, move to, and search commands to specify objects for deletion. The same technique can be applied to other commands that modify the editing buffer, such as those in the next section.

4.3 Changes, Replacements, and Substitutions

vi offers three related sets of commands for the modification of existing text. All of them use a combination of text deletion and insertion to achieve the desired result.

```
Change text (ncOBJtextESC
```

The commands to change text require that an object be specified to indicate the scope of the change. Any of the text objects just described may be used with the change command. For example, **2cwnew textESC** tells v i to change two words to the phrase "new text". If the cursor is at the beginning of a word, then two whole words are changed to the "new text". If the cursor is within a word (including the space separating it from the next word), only the part of the word between the cursor and its end is affected.

If the change to be made affects only the current line, v i marks the start of the change with the cursor at its current position and places a $ at the end of the affected text region. If the new text occupies more or less space than that being replaced, v i adjusts accordingly, showing what is happening on the screen. The effect of a change command is a deletion of existing text followed by an insertion of new text. However, the text being deleted stays on the screen until it is overwritten or until the terminating **ESC** is typed.

If a change command's scope extends beyond the current line, the affected text region is simply deleted and v i treats your subsequent input as a standard text insertion.

For the change example just cited, the sequence looks like this.

Before:

```
                                              SCREEN DATA
Here is some old information.
```

After the **2cw** part of the command is issued:

```
                                              SCREEN DATA
Here is some old informatio$.
```

After the command completes:

```
                                              SCREEN DATA
Here is some new text.
```

Doubling the command letter causes the basic command to operate on whole lines. Therefore, **cc** changes the current line and **ncc** changes **n** lines starting with the current line.

Change to End of Line (**cn$** or **nC**)

The **C** command, a synonym for **c$**, deletes text to the end of the current line and then inserts new text in its place. An optional count **n**, which may be placed before or after the **c** in the **c$** form of the command, makes the change effective to the end of the **n**th line, including the current line. Multiline changes cause the text to be deleted from the buffer and the screen—no mark is used to show the extent of the change.

Substitute text (**nstextESC** or **nStextESC**)

---

vi will let you substitute a text string of any reasonable length for one or more existing characters. The substitute command effectively deletes the number of characters specified by a preceding count (the default is one) and inserts the new text. So the command **sr by the minute ESC** alters the meaning of the following sentence slightly.

Before:

SCREEN DATA

```
It's getting late_and I'm still not done.
```

After:

SCREEN DATA

```
It's getting later by the minute_and I'm still
not done.
```

The **S** command, a synonym for **cc**, replaces the current line with whatever new text is typed in. As usual, a preceding count may be used to tell *vi* how many objects, in this case lines, are affected.

Replace text (***nrc*** *or* ***RtextESC***)

To replace a single character, type **r** followed by the replacement character. Thus, **rb** will replace the character at the cursor position with the letter "b". This is a self-terminating command—it knows that only one character is being substituted in place of another, so there is no need to type **ESC**. If you do, v i will issue a warning, but no harm is done.

A handy way to split a long line into shorter lines is to find a space character in the interior of the line and type **r<CR>**, which replaces the space with a newline character. UNIX uses a single new line to delimit lines in text files. It automatically converts the carriage return you type into a new line in the editing buffer.

If a count, ***n***, is given to the **r** command, each of the next ***n*** characters will be replaced by the specified character. If less than ***n*** characters remain between the cursor position and the end of the line, no replacement takes place, and an error is signaled.

Replacement of a series of characters is achieved with the **R** command. This command is v i's overtype function, which puts each character you type in the place of the character at the cursor position, then it moves the cursor one position to the right. To signal the end of the inserted text, press **ESC**. This command uses the preceding count to repeat the replace ***n*** times. If you type **2R---ESC** in the following situation, here is what happens.

Before:

SCREEN DATA

123456789

After:

```
                                                          SCREEN DATA
  12------6789
```

The effect of this is a replacement of three characters and an *insertion* of a second copy of the new material. A similar behavior occurs when a replacement takes place at the end of a line and the new material extends beyond the original text. The overtype "mode" switches to pure text insertion at the point where the original text has all been overwritten.

———— *4.4 Copying Text* ————

Further manipulations of a text file are possible by using commands that let you move and copy text objects. Copying text involves "yanking" a copy of the source text and "putting" the copy elsewhere in the editing buffer.

```
  Yank a Copy of Text (ynOBJ)
```

The vi yank command is the electronic analogue of a photocopier. It allows you to take a copy of some specified text object and save it in the delete buffer by default or in some named buffer (described later in this lesson). Typing **y3w**, for example, copies three words, including the word containing the cursor, while leaving the original text undisturbed.

One form of the yank command has a synonym that is not a parallel for those of other commands. Whereas the commands **C** and **D** are synonyms for **c$** and **d$**, respectively, **Y** is synonymous with **yy**, the command to yank a copy of one or more full lines. **10Y** means the same thing as **10yy**, which yanks a copy of 10 lines beginning with the current line. The command **y$** yanks text from the cursor position to the end of the current line.

Put Text in Buffer (*n*p or *n*P)

The put command reverses the action of the yank and delete commands—it puts the yanked or deleted text into the editing buffer at the current cursor position. The **p** command puts the text to the right of or below the cursor, and **P** puts the text to the left of or above the cursor.

If a count is given, it is ignored by both forms of the put command if the text to be "put" is a whole line or a block of lines. However, a count will cause *n* copies of a partial-line yank or delete command to be put into the editing buffer.

When programming, it is often easier to copy some existing lines of source code and edit them than it is to type the new material completely. To copy a line in a C program you simply "yank" a copy of what you need to reproduce and "put" the copy in the new location. The following sequence of commands does the job of making a new line of code that is similar, but not identical, to one that already exists. The cursor must be somewhere in the line to be copied, but not necessarily at the beginning.

yy (yank the current line)

p (put the yanked line below the current line)

Before doing anything:

```
                                                    SCREEN DATA
#define M̲IN(ab) (((a) < (b)) ? (a) : (b))
```

After yanking the line (**yy**) and putting it (**p**):

```
                                                    SCREEN DATA
#define MIN(ab) (((a) < (b)) ? (a) : (b))
#̲define MIN(ab) (((a) < (b)) ? (a) : (b))
```

After the commands **fI**, **2sAXESC**, **f<**, and **r>**:

```
                                                    SCREEN DATA
#define MIN(ab) (((a) < (b)) ? (a) : (b))
#define MAX(ab) (((a) ≥ (b)) ? (a) : (b))
```

This is a simple example, but it shows that you can save some
keystrokes in many text entry situations, including program source
code creation. Simply saving a few keystrokes is not a high-ranking
priority of fast typists, but it is a strong incentive to the rest of us
to learn to use vi's facilities to our advantage.

4.5 Moving Text

Using a sequence of delete and put commands, you can easily
move text from one part of the editing buffer to another. The
procedure is the same for a move as for a copy, except that the
original text is deleted from the editing buffer instead of just being
replicated.

If you do several text deletions in a row, it might seem that the
earlier ones are gone for good. Not so. Lesson 6 describes some
techniques for recovering previously deleted text that might otherwise be lost.

4.6 Using Named Buffers

There are 26 buffers, named a through z, into which you may
copy or delete text.

```
Using Named Buffers ("bufynOBJ or "bufdnOBJ)
```

The first of these commands yanks text into a named buffer; the
second deletes the text object(s) into the named buffer. (That's a
double quote character starting the commands.) The optional count,

n, can be used to multiply the effective range of these commands. The commands work the same way as the yank and delete commands described earlier, except that the material is yanked or deleted into a special place in memory that you can name and use later to retrieve the text.

Any previous contents of the selected buffer are overwritten by the new material when the buffer name is typed as a lowercase letter. Typing the buffer name as an uppercase letter causes new material to be appended to anything that is already in the buffer, thus allowing you accumulate bits and pieces into one or more buffers in any order that suits your purpose.

Recover Deleted Text (*"buf***p** or *"buf***P**)

These commands retrieve previously deleted material and put it into the editing buffer either after (**p**) or before (**P**) the cursor. Therefore, **"ap** puts the contents of the named buffer "a" into the editing buffer after or below the cursor and **"aP** puts the contents of the "a" buffer to the left of or above the cursor. Partial lines in a buffer are inserted "in line", but whole lines retrieved from a buffer effectively open a new line for the insertion.

The named buffers together with the yank, delete, and put commands prove a flexible means of copying and moving text around in the editing buffer. Using our sample text file (only a few lines are shown here), the command **"xy2w** yanks two words (a partial line) into the buffer "x". Moving the cursor to the word "justice" in the editing buffer and typing **"xP** puts a copy of the contents of "x" in the editing buffer before the word "justice" with no intervening space. Since the contents of the "x" buffer are replicated in the editing buffer, not moved, "x" may be used in other put operations to sprinkle its contents about in the buffer.

Yanking two words into "x" (**/Uni<CR>**, **"xy2w**):

```
                                                    SCREEN DATA

We,
the people of the United States,
in order to form a more perfect Union,
establish justice,


```

Moving to a word (**/just<CR>**):

```
                                                    SCREEN DATA

We,
the people of the United States,
in order to form a more perfect Union,
establish justice,
...
/just
```

Putting contents of "x" into the editing buffer (**"xP**):

```
                                                    SCREEN DATA

We,
the people of the United States,
in order to form a more perfect Union,
establish United Statesjustice,


```

Of course, the transplanting of the words in this case is artificial, but it demonstrates the way named buffers are used. Had the buffer contained whole lines instead of partial lines, the text would have been put in between the current line and the line above (**P**) or below (**p**).

————————————————— Exercises ——————————————————

1. Load the "US_Cons" file for editing. Type a single command that deletes all text from the beginning of the buffer up to but not including the word "welfare". Restore the buffer by typing **:e!<CR>**.

2. Find the second occurrence of the word "States". Use the change command to change it to "STATES". Restore the buffer.

3. While you're on the word "States", use the replace command to overtype it with "STATES". Do you prefer this method to that of Exercise 2? Restore the buffer.

4. What commands do you use to split the longest line in the buffer into two parts and insert a tab at the beginning of the newly formed second part? Restore the buffer.

5. Make a copy of the first four lines of the buffer and tack the copy onto the end. What sequence of commands did you use? Restore the buffer.

6. Move the first four lines of text to the end of the buffer by using a named buffer. What commands did you use? Abandon the editing changes to the buffer and quit **vi**.

Using
5 | Insert-Mode
Commands

Goals

—Learn to correct mistakes during inserts

—Use special insert-mode commands and options

—Alter the meanings of commands and special characters

As we have discovered, there are many ways to enter the visual insert mode. While you are entering text, additional commands are available that can help you to correct input errors, do simple formatting operations, and alter the meaning of selected characters.

— 5.1 Error-Correcting Commands —

If, while entering text, you make typing errors or change your mind about a choice of words, you can quickly and easily correct or change your input with the following commands. These three commands move the cursor back over text from the current insertion point by one or more characters. In all cases, the inserted text remains displayed on the screen until you overtype it or leave the insert mode. But it is removed immediately from the editing buffer.

Erase previous character (**<BS>** or **^H**)

The backspace key, **<BS>**, regardless of how it is labeled on your computer or terminal, causes **vi** to back up one character position. Although the character remains visible in the display window, it is removed from the editing buffer. By pressing the **<BS>** key, you can erase characters one at a time all the way back to the beginning of the current input or current line, whichever comes first. **vi** does not backspace across line boundaries, and it will not back up further than the start of current input.

On terminals that have no specially labeled key to perform the backspace function, you can use the **^H** combination instead. Touch typists usually prefer the latter method because it is not necessary to hunt for a special key that has no standardized position on the keyboard.

Erase current or previous word (**^W**)

To erase from the cursor position back to the beginning of the current word, use **^W**. Repeated use of the command continues movement backward one word at a time until the beginning of the current insert or the beginning of the current line is reached, whichever comes first. **^W** does not wrap around line boundaries. It uses embedded punctuation marks as word delimiters (like **b** in visual command mode).

An example of the effect of successive applications of **^W** follows. While backing the cursor along the line one word at a time, **vi** leaves the characters it passes over on the screen. If you press the **ESC** key at any point, the text to the right of the cursor position is lost. If you type in new text, it displays over any characters left on the screen by the "erase word" command.

SCREEN DATA

This is some text I d̲idn'̲t m̲ean t̲o type.__

. . .

Erase current input or line (@)

To erase back to the start of the current insertion (or to the beginning of the current line if the insertion fills one or more lines on the screen), type the line-kill character. This is often @ on older UNIX systems, but the character may be changed by you for your own working environment (or by the system administrator for all users) by using the UNIX **stty** command. Some microcomputer versions of the UNIX system (XENIX is one) use ^U for the default line-kill character.

– 5.2 *Special Insert-Mode Commands* –

Several formatting commands may be used in visual insert mode. These help you to achieve the desired look or arrangement you want for such items as program source code files, simple documents that will not receive further automatic processing, and columnar tables.

Horizontal tab (^I or **<TAB>**)

This is the default tab provided by most computer systems and terminals. The UNIX system default tabstop is set at every eighth column beginning with the first, but v i lets you set this to other values. Such changes have an effect only within. Outside the editor, a tab inserted by v i is treated like any other tab. It is not possible with v i to set and clear individual tabs. Tabs always occur at multiples of the basic tabbing interval.

An editor variable called **tabstop** holds the current tabbing interval value. The **tabstop** variable is another of the editor configuration variables that may be viewed and altered by using the **set** command of the line editor. The variable name may be abbreviated to **ts**. Lesson 8 contains details about configuring the editor using **set** and editor variables.

You can compress the on-screen appearance of tabbed material by setting a smaller tabbing interval, say four, so that indented lines in a source list fit better in the display window. If you save the buffer to a disk file and print it out, the tabs will resume their normal values set by the UNIX defaults or by programs that establish special tab settings.

Shift by "Shiftwidth" (**^T**)

This command also performs a horizontal shifting operation by using a value stored in the **shiftwidth** variable to determine where to move the cursor. The default **shiftwidth** (or simply **sw**) is eight columns, just like **tabstop**, but many programmers like to use an indentation of three or four columns to keep their structured source code from creeping off the right side of the terminal or computer screen and the printed page.

If **shiftwidth** and **tabstop** have are equal, then **^T** behaves identically to **^I**—it inserts a tab. However, setting a value into **shiftwidth** that differs from **tabstop** causes the editor to create a shift composed of spaces, tabs, or a combination of the two. If you assume the default **tabstop** of eight, setting a **shiftwidth** of four, for example, means that a shift at the left margin will be made up of four spaces, two shifts in a row will be replaced by a tab, and so on.

The editor has an optional "autoindent" feature that automatically provides indentation for new lines during text insertion to the indentation of the previous line. You can activate the autoindent feature by typing **:set autoindent<CR>** from within the **vi** editor or by placing the line **set autoindent** in an editor startup file or in an EXINIT variable. (*See* Appendix B for details about customizing the editor.) The name of the feature can be abbreviated to **ai**.

Backtab over autoindent (**^D** or **0^D**)

The autoindent feature of the editor, when active, automatically indents new text lines to match the level of indentation of the line from which the insert was initiated. This feature is particularly useful to programmers writing program source code where indentation is visually helpful to readers of the program. It is also useful to writers for creating blocked text, "hanging indents", and other visual effects without the aid of a text formatter.

If you need to start a new line further to the left than the autoindent position, then, override the autoindent by typing ^D. Each ^D command moves the cursor left by one shiftwidth. To disregard all of the autoindentation, type 0^D. These commands are effective only if used immediately after vi supplies automatic indentation.

The line numbers in square brackets in the display simulations refer to the descriptions accompanying the sequence of frames that follow. The **tabstop** and **shiftwidth** variables should both be set to the default of eight for this example. We start by creating the first line [1], which has a leading tab.

```
                                                    SCREEN DATA
[1]     / * find the end of the string */
[2]     __
```

As soon as the **<CR>** is typed to end the line, the cursor goes to the next line and moves to the same column as the first visible character on the line above. To get the same indentation level, just type the text of the next line. Again, when the return key is typed, the cursor will go to the same indentation level on the next line.

```
                                                    SCREEN DATA
[1]      / * find the end of the string */
[2]      while ( *cp)
[3]      __
```

This time, you want to indent the text one additional level, so the first character to type is a tab, then the text of the line. The next line will be indented to this new level, which is one beyond what is needed for the next statement in the program.

```
                                                          SCREEN DATA
  [1]      / * find the end of the string */
  [2]      while ( *cp)
  [3]           ++cp;
  [4]      —
```

The "backtab" command comes into play now. Typing ^D moves the cursor back one shiftwidth, which is the same as a tabstop for this example. This backs up the cursor to align the next line typed with those above the previous line. Here's how the formatted source code fragment looks.

```
                                                          SCREEN DATA
  [1]      / * find the end of the string */
  [2]      while ( *cp)
  [3]           ++cp;
  [4]      return (cp–s);
```

It is unfortunate that vi has command names that have different meanings in different modes. There just are not enough keys on most keyboards to permit unique and mnemonic names for everything.

```
  Interrupt the editor (<Del>, <Rub>)
```

Several editing tasks are potentially time consuming and might need to be terminated prematurely. A string search is a good example. When you type a command like **/find me!ESC**, the editor searches through the editing buffer for "find me!". While searching in visual mode, the editor places the cursor at the beginning of the status line to indicate to you that it is doing something.

You can use the **<Del>** (or **<Rub>**) key to interrupt such activities. Perhaps you typed the wrong search string or simply changed your mind. Rather than wait for vi to conclude the search, which in a large buffer could take many seconds, type **<Del>** or **<Rub>** to terminate the search and return to the place in the editing buffer where the search was started.

—— *5.3 Quoting Special Characters* ——

You may need to insert special characters into a file. Such characters usually are nonprinting and have significance to v i. To put a special character, sometimes called a "meta-character" into the editing buffer requires telling v i to turn off the special meaning temporarily. Here is how it's done.

Quote erase and kill characters (\\)

The character erase (backspace —^H) and line-kill (@ or as specified) characters can be quoted to remove their special meanings by preceding them with a backslash (\\). The sequence \\^H leaves a literal backspace character in the buffer and it is visually represented on screen by a two-character ^H symbol (caret plus "H") that *vi* treats internally as one character (ASCII 8, control-h). This use of the backslash to alter the meaning of a character is sometimes called an "escape".

To see the difference between a quoted control character and a typed string to simulate its visual representation, do the following. Open a line for input (**o**), and type a caret (or uparrow as it is sometimes called) followed by a capital H, and then a space or two; then type a backslash followed by a <**BS**> key or the ^H combination. Terminate the input with an **ESC**.

SCREEN DATA

^H   ^H̲

Now use the cursor keys to move back and forth across the visually equivalent symbols. The one on the left is two printable symbols, each a valid resting place for the cursor, whereas the one on the right is just a visible representation of a control character. When you try to move through it, you can land on the H but not on the ^ part of the special symbol.

Quote nonprinting characters (^V)

Any nonprinting special character can be quoted by the use of ^V as an escape mechanism. (Early versions of vi used ^Q for this purpose but that usage was in conflict with what is known as XON/ XOFF flow control.) The quoting mechanism permits, for example, the inclusion of the literal escape control character (ASCII 27, ESC) in your input, where a typed **ESC** would normally tell vi to terminate the insert mode. **ESC** is visually represented by ^[, another two-character sequence that symbolizes this single control character. This approach can be very useful when you write a UNIX shell script, for example, that must contain literal control codes. Table 5-1 lists all useable control codes, their visual representations, and descriptions of their common uses.

Table 5-1. Control Characters

ASCII Value[1]

Character	Dec	Hex	Description
NUL	000	00	Null (padding character)
SOH	001	01	Start of Header
STX	002	02	Start of Text
ETX	003	03	End of Text
EOT	004	04	End of Transmission
ENQ	005	05	Enquire
ACK	006	06	Acknowledge
BEL	007	07	Terminal Bell
BS	008	08	Backspace
HT	009	09	Horizontal Tab
LF	010	0A	Linefeed[2]
VT	011	0B	Vertical Tab
FF	012	0C	Form Feed
CR	013	0D	Carriage Return
SO	014	0E	Shift Out
SI	015	0F	Shift In
DLE	016	10	Data Link Escape
DC1	017	11	Device Control 1
DC2	018	12	Device Control 2
DC3	019	13	Device Control 3
DC4	020	14	Device Control 4
NAK	021	15	Negative Acknowledgement
SYN	022	16	Synchronous Idle
ETB	023	17	End of Transmitted Block
CAN	024	18	Cancel
EM	025	19	End of Medium
SUB	026	1A	Substitute
ESC	027	1B	Escape
FS	028	1C	File Separator
GS	029	1D	Group Separator
RS	030	1E	Record Separator
US	031	1F	Unit Separator
DEL	127	FF	Delete (Rubout)

[1] Seven-bit codes define ASCII characters, which range in value from 0 to 127 decimal (00–FF hex). Only the control codes are listed in this table.

[2] Newline for systems that use a single line-termination character instead of a combination CR/LF. (UNIX uses NL.)

———————————————— Exercises ————————————————

1. During text input, how far back can you erase characters or words if you make mistakes? Can you use a count to multiply the effect of the **<BS>** and **^W** insert-mode commands?

2. If your line-kill character is @, how can you put a literal at sign in a file you are creating? What if @ is not your line-kill character?

3. Create a file called "steps" that contains a set of three short lines, each indented one tabstop beyond the one before, and then two more lines reversing the step ("undenting" if you'll pardon the use of an unword). Something that looks like this will do:

```
                                                      SCREEN DATA

one
        two
                three
        four
five
```

Don't leave the insert mode to do this and don't edit the file afterward to achieve the effect either.

4. How can you put a literal escape character in the editing buffer if **ESC** tells **vi** to end insert mode operation?

5. For those of you who read about but did not try the control character demonstration, edit a file on a new line (by using the **o** command or something equivalent) and type in the following characters:

↑ (a caret)

an L

a horizontal tab

a control-L combination (^L)

and end input by pressing the **ESC** key.

Now use the arrow keys or their equivalent to move back and forth across the line. Describe the behavior that you observe.

Recovering from Errors

Goals

—"Undo" the effects of simple errors

—Retrieve previously deleted text

—Retrieve files "lost" due to interrupts or errors

—Recovering from "internal" editor errors

It is almost impossible to create or edit a file without some error occuring, either self-inflicted or caused by some external influence. vi provides several ways to recover from errors, each of which is tailored to a particular set of circumstances.

6.1 Undoing Commands

If you change your mind about something you did or simply make a mistake, it is easy to undo commands that alter the contents of the editing buffer.

Undo the most recent command (**u**)

Typing **u** reverses the effect of the most recent command that affected the editing buffer and restores the buffer and the display window to their former conditions. For example, if you delete 10 lines of text and realize they were the wrong 10 lines to delete, typing **u** puts them back. The **undo** command will even restore the editing buffer after global changes that possibly affect many parts of the buffer. However, the effects of only the last buffer-modifying command can be reversed.

The **undo** command also undoes an undo—it is its own inverse. If you want to compare two ways of presenting some information, you can key in version one, replace it with version two by some appropriate means, and then toggle between them by using **u** until you settle on the version you want to retain.

Restore Current Line (**U**)

If you make a series of changes to a single line, you can restore the original line by using the **U** command. It works like the **u** command except that it reverses the compound effect of more than one command, but it applies to just the current line. If you move the cursor off the line containing the changes, **U** cannot be used to reverse them. If you do move off the line and want to reverse at least the last change made, use **u**. But don't call upon **U** first because it will prevent a subsequent **u** command from working.

Unlike its lowercase sibling, the **U** command cannot be repeated. It does not undo its own action.

——— *6.2 Retrieving Deleted Lines* ———

You have already learned about the "put" command for recovering the last deleted text or "yanked" text. Used in combination with numbered buffers, the put commands become a powerful error recovery tool.

Put Previously Deleted Text (*"n*p, *"n*P)

In addition to an unnamed delete buffer, vi also has nine numbered buffers (1 through 9) into which it saves the last nine deletions of whole lines. The most recent deletion of one or more whole lines goes into the first numbered buffer, pushing the contents of the previous deletion, if any, into the second numbered buffer, and so on. The contents of the ninth numbered buffer will be lost when the tenth block of deleted lines is moved into the first numbered buffer.

To recover text from any of the numbered buffers, type a double quote and the number of the buffer, followed by a **p** (or **P**), which puts the deleted text into the editing buffer after (before) the current line. If you specify a numbered buffer that contains no text, vi displays a message on the status line: *Nothing in register N,* where N is the number you typed.

Because you may not know which numbered buffer contains the needed text, vi provides a shortcut method of examining them. Normally the repeat command (.) means repeat the previous command. When used with the numbered buffers, as in **"1pu.u.u.u**, the repeat command increments the buffer number, thus causing the contents of the next higher numbered buffer to be put into the editing buffer. Alternating repeat commands with the undo command lets you quickly cycle through the numbered buffers looking for lost data. When the ninth buffer is reached, vi continues to retrieve its contents on subsequent calls from the repeat command.

6.3 Recovering Files After Interrupts ── and Crashes ──

Sooner or later, you will be the victim of an unexpected interrupt or system crash that makes it impossible to continue with an editing session. When someone gets the system back on its feet after a crash, or when you log in again after an interrupted connection is restored, you may find mail telling you that one or more files were saved.

Typical "recover" message:

```
                                                   SCREEN DATA
A copy of an editor buffer of your file ''junk''
was saved when your phone was hung up.
This file may be retrieved using the ''recover''
command of the editor.
(etc.)
```

When you are editing, vi keeps a copy of the file in a temporary work area on disk. Under abnormal conditions, the temporary area may not be erased if there is no way to find out from you whether to update the original file. Because of this situation, you may be able to recover most of the work of an aborted editing session.

Get list of saved files (**vi -r<CR>**)

Typing **vi -r<CR>** tells vi to print a list of saved files. If there are none, vi responds with "No files saved." Otherwise, it produces a list of file names.

```
                                                   SCREEN DATA
$ vi -r
On Fri Mar 22 at 00:36 saved 511 lines of file ''lsn12''
On Sun Mar 24 at 14:10 saved 39 lines of file ''junk''
$ _
```

To recover a particular file, use the procedure described here.

Recover a file (**vi -r** *name*<CR>)

To recover a file that you know has been saved by the editor move to the directory where you want the recovered file to be placed and type **vi -r** *name*<CR> at the UNIX prompt. Wait for vi to find and load the file and then survey its contents. Use the normal commands to save changes or not—whatever is appropriate for the circumstances. It may well be that what was saved was garbage anyway. Trash it so you don't waste perfectly good disk space. For the same reason, you should not leave saved files in the temporary area any longer than necessary.

There may be more than one copy of the same file, each preserving a different state of the file from different interrupts or crashes. Using **vi -r** *name*<CR> will retrieve the most recent version of the file. To retrieve successively older versions, use this procedure repeatedly until you get the desired copy of the saved file. Each time you use the recovery procedure, vi will load the named file into the editing buffer, where you can save it in your own directory, edit it further, or ignore it (quit without saving).

6.4   *Preserving a File*

You may need to simulate a system crash sometime. If you encounter an error that makes it impossible for you to save the file you are editing, don't assume all hope is lost.

Type **:preserve**<CR> to tell vi to fake a crash (this may be abbreviated to **:pre**<CR>). The command will retain a copy of what you are editing as if a real disaster had occurred. Then you can use the recovery options to the vi command to try to get back the edited file at a time that permits saving it permanently in a safe place that you control. (Technical note: It is often the case that this problem occurs when you try to write a file on a file system for which you have read-only permission. This is a frequent problem on multiple computer systems that have cross-connected file systems.)

6.5   *Refreshing the Screen*

Several situations may develop in which the screen needs to be refreshed to improve its readability. The first situation has to do with external messages being displayed; the second situation is screen clutter caused by the way the editor works on some terminals.

These are not errors, but the screen appearance may be such that you can't figure out where the cursor is. Each of the following commands has a special purpose.

Clear and Redraw Screen (^L)

Messages from other users (which they send to you by using the UNIX system's **write** command) or from tasks running in the background may clutter the screen, causing it to no longer reflect accurately what is in the editing buffer. (The editing buffer itself is not disturbed by such incoming messages.) Type ^L (an ASCII formfeed) to clear the screen and redraw it from the editing buffer.

On occasion, you may have electrical noise on the communications link to your terminal that alters the appearance of the screen and that may also put vi into an unknown state. This is an error condition. The first thing to do is to press the **ESC** key one or more times until you here a warning tone or see the screen flash. The ^L command can then be used to redraw the display screen.

Redraw Screen (^R)

On dumb video terminals, deleted lines are indicated by an @ symbol at the left margin. This lets vi respond to your changes quickly, even at slow transmission rates, but it fouls the screen with useless empty lines. Also, on any terminal, a line of text that is too long to fit on the screen will be replaced by a lone @ symbol.

To eliminate these empty lines that are "forgotten but not gone" and thus permitting more lines from the editing buffer to be displayed, type ^R. Unlike the ^L command, ^R does not clear the screen. It simply redraws the screen from the point of the first deleted line, possibly saving some time, which is important on terminals connected via slow transmission circuits.

6.6 Recovering from Internal Editor Errors

Certain situations occur that even the vi editor finds hopeless and distressing. When this happens, vi will display a message, possibly informative, more likely not, and switch to the ex command mode of the editor. The ex command mode will be activated if you accidentally type **Q** while in vi command mode, too. Later, we'll explore why you may want to do this on purpose.

If you find yourself in ex command mode [signaled by a colon prompt (:)] and you want to continue editing in vi, type **:vi<CR>** to return to the previous editing context, or as close to it as vi can get. Alternately, you can quit the editor and restart. Some users feel this is a safer way to recover from an unknown error.

To quit editing, use any of the ex commands you have already learned to save changes and quit or to abandon changes. All of the ex commands for this will work; but, ex knows nothing about the **ZZ** command.

Exercises

1. In a file of your choosing, use the **dd** command and a companion **p** command to move two lines from the beginning of the editing buffer to somewhere in the interior. Use the **u** command to reverse the operation. How much of the operation is undone? Now use the **dd** and **p** commands to restore the file to its original condition.

2. Type **:preserve<CR>** to see how vi simulates a crash, which forces the editing buffer to be saved. Exit to the UNIX shell and go through the complete file recovery procedure starting with a list of saved files. (On most UNIX systems, you'll have mail telling you about it.)

3. If you can, have someone send a message (using the **write** command) to you while you are editing a file. Use ^L to redraw the screen to clean up the mess. Would ^R have the same effect?

4. Edit any file you wish in the following way. Delete the first two words, then delete a line of text, then delete another two lines. What simple command can you use for that last operation? Can you get back all of the deleted text? If not, what portion of deleted material can you restore.

Working with Files

Goals

—Read text from other files into the editing buffer

—Collect the output of UNIX shell commands into the editing buffer

—Write selected portions of the buffer to a file

—Move blocks of text within an editing buffer

—Use the current and alternate editing buffers to transfer text between files

—Edit files in sequence

The vi editor, like all other text editors for the UNIX system, interacts intimately with the UNIX file system. The operations of reading and writing files are of primary importance.

———— 7.1 Writing to a File ————

We have already seen how to write the contents of the editing buffer to a file in permanent storage by using the **:w<CR>**

command. Several variations of the write command give you added flexibility in saving text and creating and updating files.

Write to a named file (**:w** *file*<**CR**>)

Without a named file, **vi** interprets this command to mean update the contents of the remembered file to match the current editing buffer contents. When a name is given, as in **:w output**<**CR**>, **vi** creates a new file and saves the buffer contents in it. The name of the remembered file is not changed, but the editor retains the name of the file you typed (**output** in this example) as an alternate file. (We'll look more closely at alternate files shortly.)

If the file already exists, you will have to tell the editor explicitly to overwrite it by typing **:w! output**<**CR**>. The file name may be a full or relative pathname.

Write lines to a named file (**:***addr1,addr2***w** *file*<**CR**>)

It is possible to write only a portion of the editing buffer to a file. Using the optional line numbers (addresses) ***addr1*** and ***addr2***, you can tell **vi** to write the lines in the range ***addr1*** to ***addr2*** inclusive to the named file or to the remembered file by default. Again, the optional **!** may be needed to overwrite an existing file.

The addresses may be specified in a very general way. They can be formed with search patterns (***/str1/,/str2/***), arithmetic based on the current line (**.-5,+10**), and so on. Lesson 10 describes addressing primitives and covers this topic more fully.

7.2   *Reading from a File or Command*
Output

vi lets you read a file at any time (you must have read permission) and put its contents into the editing buffer after the current line. It also lets you take the output of a UNIX command as input into the editing buffer.

Read from a file (**:r** *file*<**CR**>)

To import information from another file into the editing buffer, type **:r** followed by the file name (full and relative pathnames and shell metacharacters are allowed) and a <**CR**>. The whitespace between the r and the file name is mandatory. A copy of the contents of the named file will be placed in the buffer following the current line.

Before:

```
                                                          SCREEN DATA

   ~
   ~
   .
   .
   .
   ~
   ~
 :r US__Cons__
```

After:

```
                                                          SCREEN DATA

We,
the people of the United States,
in order to form a more perfect Union,
establish justice,
insure domestic tranquility,
provide for the common defense,
promote the general welfare,
and secure the blessings of liberty to
ourselves and our posterity,
do ordain and establish this
Constitution for
the United States of America.


~
~
~

14 new lines
```

Notice the blank line at the top of the editing buffer. The blank line occurs because a "read" command appends new text after the current line, even if it is empty. This technique can be used to read the contents of any accessible text file into the editing buffer.

Read from a command (:r !*cmd*<CR> or *n*!!*cmd*<CR>)

If you want to include the output of an external command in the editing buffer, use the **read** command in conjunction with a temporary "shell escape" which is an invocation of another user shell without leaving the editor (Shell escapes are covered in a general way in the next lesson). To put a large headline in a file, for example, you could take the output of the UNIX banner command and read it into the buffer. Typing **:r !banner MEETING NOTICE<CR>** produces the effect shown in Figure 7-1.

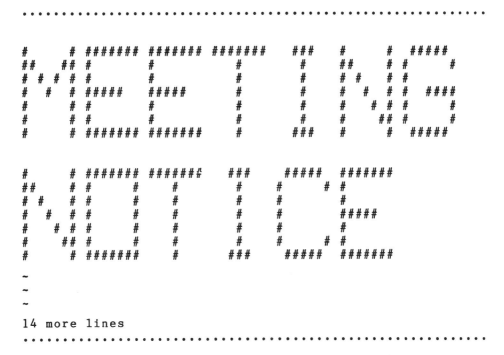

Figure 7-1. Reading output of a command into the buffer.

Reading the date and time into the editing buffer is a simple matter. Typing **:r !date<CR>** places the date and time in the buffer on the line below the current line, pushing any existing lines down the screen.

The other form of read command replaces **n** lines (one by default) with the command output. When you type the count, **n**, and the first !, neither is displayed anywhere on the screen. The second ! you type causes **vi** to display ! on the last line of the screen where it then awaits the command to be run.

An example of this command in use is the following, which shows a document being prepared that contains a list of the files that make it up. To be sure the list is up to date, a marker is placed in the file. When the document is being assembled, the line with the reminder message is replaced by a current list obtained from the UNIX **ls** command.

Before:

```
                                                        SCREEN DATA
 .
 .
 .
Here is a listing of the current directory, which
contains the files needed to build this document.
[ * * insert current list here * *]
```

The command **‼ls<CR>** instructs vi to replace the current line (no count given, so only one line is changed) with the output of the command.

After:

```
                                                        SCREEN DATA
 .
 .
 .
Here is a listing of the current directory, which
contains the files needed to build this document.
cover
intro
lsn01
lsn02
lsn03
20 more lines
```

Again, the last line informs you of the extent of the operation's effect on the editing buffer. Only a few could fit in the display window, but the rest are in the buffer, which may be scrolled down to bring the rest of the inserted lines into view.

─────── 7.3 *Editing a File* ───────

During an editing session, you may want to edit another file or begin reediting the current file. The **ex** edit command, **e**, initiates the editing process. It has several variations.

Reedit current file (**:e!<CR>**)

If some changes have been made to the editing buffer and you decide not to keep them, you can start fresh with the same file by typing **:e!<CR>**. This results in the contents of the remembered disk file being read into the editing buffer, replacing the unwanted edited version in the buffer. The cursor will be placed on the first line of the buffer, where you can begin editing anew. Try to get it right this time.

Edit a file (**:e** *file*<CR> or **:e!** *file*<CR>)

If the edit command includes a file name, **vi** will begin editing the named file provided there are no unwritten changes in the editing buffer. If unwritten changes exist, you will be told and asked to save them before proceeding, or to use the alternate form of the command, **:e!** *file*<CR>, which ignores changes.

─────── 7.4 *Alternate File Editing* ───────

Although **vi** does not include split-screen editing or windowing of editing buffers, it allows two files to be edited alternately. **vi** lets you operate on only one file at a time, but it can remember the names of a "current" file and an "alternate" file and manage two main editing buffers simultaneously.

The name of the current file is saved in a variable called %, and that of the alternate file is saved in #. You can use the full names of the files you are editing, but these shorthand notations can save lots of typing.

Current File (%)

The current file name symbol has several primary uses. If you do want to find out what the permissions are for the current file, you can use a temporary shell escape. Type **:!ls -l %<CR>** to see a one-line long directory listing for the current file. The % will be immediately expanded to the name used to specify the current disk file and the **ls -l** command handed to a subshell for execution. You will be prompted to type **<CR>** to return to editing when the operation completes.

In the next lesson, you will see how % is used with other UNIX commands to specify that operations should be performed on the current disk file.

Alternate File (#)

Anytime another file is named for reading or writing, **vi** remembers its name as the alternate file. To edit the alternate file, if one is known to **vi**, type **:e #<CR>**. (Use **:e! #<CR>** if the current buffer contains unwritten changes that you want to abandon.) After this command has executed, the alternate becomes the current file, and *vise versa*.

One use of this feature involves reading a copy of the alternate file into the editing buffer, which by definition contains a copy of the current file. Move the cursor to the line after which you want the new text to be placed and type **:r #<CR>**. That's all there is to it. No need to type out a complete pathname for the alternate file because **vi** already knows it.

7.5   *Transferring Text Between*
Buffers

In Lesson 4 you learned about several ways to copy or move text from one part of the editing buffer to another. It is possible, using similar techniques, to copy or move text from one editing buffer to another.

Both copying and moving text between editing buffers are important capabilities for programmers and wordsmiths alike. The secret lies in using named buffers to store the material to be transferred. You may want to review Lesson 4, especially the part about using named buffers, before proceeding.

Copy Text

Copying text leaves the original material in its buffer and places a copy of it in the alternate buffer. The yank and put commands do all the work by using a named buffer for temporary storage. (Numbered buffers will not work because their contents are lost when editing buffers are switched.)

To copy text between buffers:

1. Yank text to a named buffer (**"xynOBJ** or **"xnyy**)

2. Swap the editing buffers (**:e #<CR>** or **:e#<CR>**)

3. Put text into the receiving editing buffer (**"xp** or **"xP**)

These commands must be used in the sequence shown. The command to yank whole lines (**yy**) may be abbreviated to **Y**. Using a text object to specify the range of the copy command is more general than operating on whole lines, but it requires a bit more care in its use. Typically, an object would be a search string, a screen position, or one of the symbols for a word, sentence, paragraph, or a larger text object.

The put command has enough flexibility that the copied text can be placed anywhere in the receiving buffer, from ahead of the first line to beyond the last line, depending on whether the **P** or **p** form is used.

To illustrate, let's copy some text from the current file into the alternate file. The current file, by definition the file you are editing on the screen, contains a sentence just right for another document you are creating. For this example, let's call the current file "source" and the alternate file "destination". For the moment, "destination" does not exist—it will be created.

Current file:

```
                                                        SCREEN DATA

   The vi editor has many commands—too many
according to some users.
   But only a handful of them are considered
essential. The commands to move the cursor
(h, j, k, l), insert and append text (i and a),
delete a character and a line (x and dd), and
a few for file management (ZZ, :q!, etc.) are the
bare minimum. All the rest are useful but not
essential.
```

To copy the second sentence into the alternate file editing buffer, first make a copy of it in a named buffer. Place the cursor at the beginning of the sentence, as just shown. Then type the command **"ay)**, which yanks a copy of the entire sentence. Switch to the alternate file by typing **:e destination<CR>** and then wait a few seconds while vi switches buffers.

```
                                                        SCREEN DATA

  —
  ~
  ~
  ~
''destination [New file]
```

Older versions of **vi** will respond with the message

''destination'' No such file or directory

which means the same thing. Now use the "put" command to insert a copy of the sentence in this buffer. Typing **"ap** will place a copy of the sentence in the editing buffer starting at the cursor position.

```
                                               SCREEN DATA
The commands to move the cursor
(h, j, k, l), insert and append text (i and a),
delete a character and a line (x and dd), and
a few for file management (ZZ, :q!, etc.) are the
bare minimum.
~
5 lines
```

The message "5 lines" on the status line tells you that vi has transferred all or part of five text lines from one file to another. This is the report feature at work. You can set the report level by using the command **:set report=**n**<CR>** so that vi will notify you when editing operations that change the buffer affect more than n lines. If you want the copied lines to remain in the destination file, you have to save it with some form of the **:w** command or **ZZ**.

Move Text

Moving text implies deleting it from the source buffer and putting the deleted material into the receiving buffer. When the buffers are written out to disk, you have effectively moved text from one file to another.

To move text between buffers:

1. Delete text into buffer (**"**x**d**n**OBJ** or **"**x**ndd**)
2. Write (or abandon) the changes (**:w<CR>** or **:w!<CR>**)
3. Swap editing buffers (**:e #<CR>** or **:e#<CR>**)
4. Put text in the receiving buffer (**"**x**p** or **"**x**P**)

This is very similar to the copy command set. However, the first command in this case deletes the text from the source buffer, and, therefore, the buffer must be saved (or changes abandoned) before you can switch to the other buffer. In all other respects it behaves in the same way as a buffer-to-buffer copy operation.

——— *7.6 Sequential Editing* ———

vi retains a list of file names in an "argument list". If vi is initially started from the UNIX command line with a set of file names (one or more), the names are saved. You can also give vi an entirely new argument list without leaving the editor.

List remembered file names (**:args<CR>**)

Advance to the next file (**:n<CR>** or **:n!<CR>**)

Rewind argument list (**:rew<CR>** or **:rewind!<CR>**)

Create new argument list (**:n** *file...***<CR>**)

The argument list has some interesting uses. Typing **:args<CR>** tells vi to display the argument list. The display starts on the last line of the screen and continues onto additional lines by scrolling the screen if necessary for a long list. If one of the files in the list is the current file, its name is bracketed (between [and]). If the current file is not one from the list (file selected directly using the **:e** *file*<CR> command), none of the names is bracketed. As you can see, it is not necessary for the current and alternate file names to be part of the argument list, although they usually are.

When you are ready to edit the next file on the list, type **:n<CR>** or **:n!<CR>**. The next file in the argument list becomes the current file name. The first of these command forms will complain if there are any unwritten changes in the editing buffer. The second command won't.

To "rewind" the file list, type **:rew<CR>** (or **:rew!<CR>** to account for a modified buffer). This command makes the first name in the argument list become the current file. Subsequent uses of **:n<CR>** will traverse the list one file at a time as just explained.

Here is an example that uses a sample directory of program source files to show how the vi argument list feature works. Assume that you need to edit a series of C files named file1.c through file4.c and that you are in the directory where these files reside.

The UNIX command line:

```
                                                    SCREEN DATA
$ vi file?.c<CR>
```

The response to **:args<CR>**:

```
                                                    SCREEN DATA
~

~
[file1.c] file2.c file3.c file4.c
```

The brackets around file1.c indicate that it is the current file, which means it is in the editing buffer. The other files are known by name only at this point; but, they are not currently being edited. Typing **:n<CR>** will cause vi to mark file1.c as the alternate file and load file2.c in as the current file. A second call to **:args<CR>** produces this result.

```
                                                    SCREEN DATA
~

~
file1.c [file2.c] file3.c file4.c
```

To create a new argument list or replace an existing one without leaving the editor, use the next (**:n**) command with a list of file names. This list becomes the argument list and the previous list, if any, is forgotten by vi. Ambiguous characters may be used to form file names just as I did in the invocation from the shell in the previous example.

—————————— Exercises ——————————

1. Create a new file named "const". Use the commands you learned in this lesson to place a banner-style heading, "CONSTI-TUTION" at the head of the file, and then read in the text of the file "US_Cons". Save the new file, but don't leave the editor. What commands do this most efficiently?

2. Copy the lines containing the banner produced in Exercise 1 into an editing buffer called "headline" by using a named buffer for temporary storage. Save the new file and continue editing. What commands are needed to do this?

3. How would you tack a list of the files in the current directory onto the end of the buffer you are now editing? Abandon changes and leave vi.

4. For this exercise, you should move to a directory that has only standard ASCII text files in it. Type a command that starts vi and brings a list of all files in the directory in as arguments. What is the command. After vi has read in the first of the files, type :args<CR> to see the argument list. (You will have to type <CR> to return to editing if the list spans more than a single screen line.)

5. Switch to the next file on the list. The next. And one more. Type :args<CR> again and notice how the brackets have moved to indicate the current file name. Now rewind the list.

LESSON 8

Editor Variables, Command Lines, and Shells

Goals

—Set variables that control the behavior of vi commands

—Use UNIX command lines effectively for starting an editing session

—Use shell escapes to expand editing capabilities and improve productivity

—Use UNIX filters to process text within the editing buffer

———— 8.1 *vi Editor Variables* ————

vi has a set of variables that store the essential information about the editor configuration and operating characteristics. There is a default set of values, but each user is free to alter the editor setting to suit personal preferences and special needs.

Table 8-1 is a list of editor variables and their default values. An editor variable may have a numeric value, a character string value, or a Boolean (on/off) value. The acceptable abbreviations and default values of each variable are listed in the table along with a brief description of each.

Table 8-1. Editor Variables.

Name	Default	Description
autoindent	noai	Leading whitespace supplied automatically
autoprint	ap	In line-editing mode, causes current line to be displayed after each delete, copy, join, move, substitute, undo, and shift command.
autowrite	noaw	Write automatically when a **:next, :tag, !, ^]**, or **^↑** command is issued.
beautify	nobf	Discard most control characters during text inserts (except tab, newline, and formfeed).
directory	dir=/tmp	Names the directory in which **ex/vi** places its editing buffer file.
edcompatible	noedcompatible	Causes behavior of substitute command suffixes to work like those of the **ed** editor.
errorbells	eb	Error messages are accompanied by a terminal bell. In visual mode, standout mode is used to highlight messages.

(Table 8.1. Continued.)

Name	Default	Description
hardtabs	ht=8	Describes the hardware tab settings of the terminal or as the host system expands tabs.
ignorecase	noic	Do "caseless" searches.
lisp	nolisp	Use (,), {, and } to move over S expressions in LISP programs.
list	nolist	Show selected control characters (^I for tab, $ for newline).
magic	nomagic	Treat ., [, and * characters as special in scanning operations.
mapinput	mi	Permits macros to be expanded in both visual command mode and visual text insertion mode.
number	nonu	Display relative line numbers.
open	open	Prevents users of the edit version of ex from entering visual and open modes.
optimize	opt	Speeds display operations of terminals that have no direct cursor addressing.
paragraphs	para=ILLPPPQPbpP LI	Name formatter macro that signal a start of paragraph. (Yes, that's a P followed by a space near the end.)

(Table 8.1. Continued.)

Name	Default	Description
prompt	prompt	Command-mode input is solicited by a colon prompt.
redraw	nore	Emulates an intelligent terminal on a dumb terminal.
report	report=5	Sets the affected-line count threshold for commands.
scroll	scroll=12	Sets number of lines that are scrolled when a scroll command is received.
sections	sect=NHSHH HU	Name text Formatter macros that signal the start of a section.
shell	sh=/bin/sh	Gives the pathname of the shell used during "shell escapes".
shiftwidth	sw=8	Distance to shift for < and > commands and for ^T and ^D during input.
showmode	noshowmode	Displays editor mode messages.
showmatch	nosm	Point to matching (when a) is typed — ditto for { and }.
slowopen	slow	Delay display updates during text inserts.
tabstop	ts=8	Sets the editor tabstop value used only for display purposes.
term	(read from env.)	Identifies the user's terminal type.

(Table 8.1. Continued.)

Name	Default	Description
terse	noterse	Tells editor to use shorter error messages.
window	window=23	Specifies the number of lines in the display window for the z and visual-mode commands.
wrapscan	ws	Searches wrap around buffer start/end boundaries.
wrapmargin	wm=0	Automatically starts a new line when a space is typed within wm of right edge of the screen.
writeany	nowa	Allows the editor to save the buffer contents to any writeable file with complaint.

View editor variables (**:set<CR>** or **:set all<CR>**)

View a specified variable (**:set** *VAR***?<CR>**)

Set an editor variable (**:set** *VAR***<CR>**)

To see an abbreviated version of the current settings of the editor variables, type **:set<CR>**. A brief line or two will be displayed at the bottom of the screen to show the values of only those variables that differ from the defaults. To get a complete listing of all editor variables and their values, type **:set all<CR>**. When you have satisfied your curiosity, type **<CR>** to return to the previous editing context.

You can view the value of a specified variable by typing **:set** *VAR***?<CR>**. The question mark is needed only for boolean variables to preclude setting the variable instead of viewing it. String and numeric variables do not have this ambiguity.

If you want to change any of the variables, you can type a set command in one of the following forms:

Option Type	Form of set command	Function
Boolean	:set *VAR*<CR>	set variable ON
	:set no*VAR*<CR>	set variable OFF
numeric	:set *VAR=number*<CR>	assign number
string	:set *VAR=str*<CR>	assign string

For example, to set a new value for the **report** level, use the command **:set report=2<CR>**. This tells the editor to display a message on the status line any time more than two lines of the buffer are affected by your editing.

8.2 UNIX Command-Line Options
for vi

The UNIX command line used to start the vi editor has numerous options that can be used to set initial conditions, override default values, and control other aspects of the editing session. Here is the general form of a vi invocation command line.

vi [*option...*] [*+command*] [*file...*]<CR>

where "option..." with noted exceptions, may be one or more of the following, either grouped or separately stated, in any order. Options requiring an argument (like **-w*n***) must be last if grouped with other options.

Option	Description
-l	Sets the showmatch and lisp options.
-r	Used to recover files saved by vi or other UNIX editors after an interrupt or system crash. If no file names are specified, tells vi to display a list of saved files.
-t*tag*	Edit the file named by the designated tag in the tags file, if any, and place the cursor on the line containing the defined tag item.
-w*n*	Set the initial window size to *n* lines.
-x	Instructs vi to ask for a file encryption/decryption key.
-R	Causes vi to operate in "readonly" mode. On some systems, this is equivalent to invoking the "view" variant of the editor.

The optional *command* argument to the **+** option may be a cursor positioning sequence that instructs vi to seek a specified line in the editing buffer after a file has been copied in. If no file is named, this optional command is useless. Examples of acceptable command arguments are summarized here:

Argument	Positions cursor to:
(none)	the end of the editing buffer
n	line *n*
/*text*	the line containing the specified text string

If the vi invocation command line has no options, commands, or file names, vi opens an empty, unnamed editing buffer analogous to a painter's pristine canvas.

8.3 Types of Shell Escapes

There will be times when you will want to return to the UNIX shell while you are editing a file to use one of the many application programs—to update a calendar, check your mail, and so on—or to use a UNIX filter program to process a portion of the editing buffer. The vi editor provides convenient ways to do this without forcing you to leave the editor.

Two types of temporary "shell escapes" are available. The first allows you to execute a single UNIX command line. The second creates a subshell for an indefinite time.

Execute a command (:*!cmd*<CR>)

Escape to subshell (:sh<CR>)

The ability to execute commands from within a running program is a convenience offered by many UNIX system programs. vi is no exception, but it is more flexible than most programs in the way it handles shell escapes.

The first form runs a command one time and then prompts you to "hit" the return key to continue. A light press will do on most keyboards; there's no need to be brutal. Most other keys (except the colon) will have the same effect as the return key. To run the date command, for example, type :!date<CR>, and vi will execute the command in a subshell and display the results at the bottom of the screen, like this:

```
                                                      SCREEN DATA
  ~

  ~

  ~

  :!date
  Sun Feb 24 12:31:37 MST 1985
  [Hit return to continue]
```

If you do press the return key after the command completes, vi redraws the screen and returns the cursor to the exact position in the editing buffer that it had when the shell escape was started. If you wish to run another command, type a colon to get to the ex command line again and give it your orders. Eventually, you will have to return to the current buffer, but you can string commands back-to-back like this if you want to.

Another example: If you are writing a document with the UNIX text processing codes and need to find out how many words it contains, type **:!deroff % | wc<CR>** and the line, word, and character totals for the current file will appear at the bottom of the screen. Be sure you have saved changes to disk if you want them reflected in these totals. The command sequence takes its input from the disk file, not from the copy in the editing buffer. (deroff is needed to take out the text processor commands that would distort the totals.)

There is an easier way to run a sequence of commands while holding your place in vi. Use the form of the shell escape that runs a subshell indefinitely. Type **:sh<CR>** to do this. vi will retain the status of the current job, but will put you into a subshell where you can work as you would in your login shell. But in this case you have at least three programs running: the login shell, the vi editor, and the current subshell.

When you are ready to return to the editor, terminate the subshell by typing **^D**. Again, vi will place the cursor exactly where it was in the editing buffer before the shell escape, and you can continue editing as if nothing had happened.

——————— *8.4 Filtering the Buffer* ———————

A means of processing text in a region of the editing buffer is provided by vi. This facilitates such tasks as sorting items in a list and converting a single-column list to multicolumn format, and so forth.

Run command on an object (**!***OBJcmd***<CR>**)

Run command on lines (**:***addr1, addr2***!***cmd***<CR>**)

The ***OBJ*** component of the first of these commands can be any of the standard text objects, but a few work best, such as paragraph boundaries or fixed positions in the editing buffer or the display window.

Here is the way to sort a list of names and display the names in two columns. Type the names in any order that they come to mind and terminate the list with a blank line. Assume you are getting ready to send out a notice for a party or meeting. Getting all of the names down is more important initially than getting them in alphabetical order. Let vi and UNIX do the hard work.

List before filtering:

The above list must now be sorted so nobody can complain about favoritism (of course they can complain about their relative positions in the alphabet, but that's a different problem).

With the cursor at the head of the list to be sorted and the end of the list marked by a blank line (or a paragraph marker recognized by vi) type **!}sort | pr -t2<CR>** and wait while vi and the UNIX filter programs do your bidding. The lines being filtered will be replaced by the output of the UNIX pipeline command.

After filtering:

```
                                                          SCREEN DATA
Bob                  Jane
Clarence             Lana
Curly                Moe
Dennis               Pete
Jake
```

NOTE:

Pre-System III UNIX systems and their derivatives have pr commands that cannot take combined arguments and that exhibit different behavior in multicolumn printing. Modifications to the commands just shown may be necessary on those systems.

The second of these buffer-filtering commands lets you specify absolute or relative line numbers or other address primitives to filter any portion of the buffer through a UNIX system command. The behavior is similar to that of the first form, but you have much better control over the portion of the editing buffer that is affected.

Other forms of filtering can be used, but be careful. This vi feature is a bit flaky and can produce some strange and unexpected results. The undo command can be used to recover from such situations if it is used before any other buffer-modifying commands are typed.

The UNIX sort and pr commands have numerous options for handling a variety of filtering chores. Many other UNIX filter programs like sed, grep, and awk can be used to alter the form of a portion of the editing buffer in some meaningful way if they are used correctly. If they are used incorrectly, you're on your own! Be safe. Before experimenting with this vi feature, be sure to save the editing buffer to disk or operate on a file that has no lasting value to you.

Don't confuse this command with a similar looking command described in Lesson 7 that has a different effect. Typing a command of the form *n!!cmd*<CR> replaces *n* lines starting at the current line with the output of the command sequence following the double exclamation points. In this case, the existing lines are deleted from the buffer, but their contents are <u>not</u> used as input to the command.

─────────────────── Exercises ───────────────────

1. Work in a directory that contains at least one text file you can edit. What command would you use to start editing a file on its last line? On the first line that contains the word "the" (assuming there is one in the file)? What happens if the string is not found?

2. What command will display a list of the files in the current directory without inserting the list in the editing buffer?

3. Escape to an indefinite subshell and try some UNIX commands. Then return to editing the file in the previous context. What commands are needed to escape and return?

4. Read in a list of files in the current directory, one name per line. (They are already sorted in ascending order by the shell.) Use a filtering command to list the file names in three columns in place of the current one-column listing. How did you do it?

Miscellaneous Commands

Goals

—Obtain editor statistics and other information about the current file

—Convert characters from one case to the other

—Join two or more lines into a single line

—Transpose out-of-order characters

—Shift and indent blocks of text lines

9.1 Editor Statistics and File Information

Several commands give you information about what is being edited.

Display status of current file (^G)

Change name of the current file (:file *file*<CR>)

You can use the ^G command at any time to get a status report on the current file. This produces a one-line summary on the status line that reports whether the file has been modified, the position of the cursor in the file, and the file's present size in lines. The status line for a sample file might look like this:

```
                                                    SCREEN DATA
''lsn09'' [Modified] line 200 of 650 --30%--
```

If the editing buffer content matches that of the file on disk, the [Modified] message does not appear, but the rest of the information is displayed. In either case, the cursor returns immediately to its position in the buffer where you can continue editing without delay.

The second of the status commands is **:file** which may be called with or without a file name. The command may be abbreviated to **:f**. Without an argument, it is a synonym for ^G. With an argument, **file**, the command changes the name of the current file to the name supplied by the argument. So typing **:f newname<CR>** tells vi to change the name of the current file to "newname". The command will produce a status report that has the following form:

```
                                                    SCREEN DATA
''newname'' [Not edited] [Modified] line 7 of 66 --10%--
```

The message "[Not edited]" is one you probably haven't seen before. It seems to conflict with the next message, "[Modified]." How can a file be modified and not edited at the same time? The confusion stems from a poor choice of words, perhaps, but here is what the messages mean.

The editor tries to protect files by preventing accidental writing to disk files that have no obvious connection to the contents of the editing buffer. Here's an example: Suppose you are editing the file "file1" and you attempt to save all or a part of the buffer to an existing file, "file2". The editor won't let you do it with a simple **:w file2<CR>** command. It requires a special assertion that tells it that you know what you are doing and that you want to replace the contents of "file2" with the contents of the editing buffer. This you do by typing **:w! file2<CR>**. Now you're responsible for the consequences, not v i. Pretty clever, huh? In this case, the editor considers "file2" to be *not edited.*

However, when you are editing a file that was named on the editor invocation command line or loaded by using **:e *file*<CR>** or a similar command, the editor considers the file to be *edited.* That means you will not have to make any special assertion to update the contents of the original file on disk.

——————— *9.2   Using Line Numbers* ———————

The visual editor lets you have numbered or unnumbered presentations of the file being edited. Sometimes line numbers get in the way, such as during table building and other tasks that fill a line on the screen. The line numbers occupy a full eight columns at the left margin, reducing the displayable text area to 72 columns on a typical 80-column screen. This apparent line-length reduction doesn't alter the editing buffer contents, but it makes it difficult to see on the screen what will be printed out on paper.

You probably use the unnumbered screen format in such cases, which is the editor's default, but you may need to know the current line number or the size of the file for use in some command.

Display line number (**:.=<CR>**)

Type **:.=<CR>** to find out the current line number or **:$=<CR>** or simply **:=<CR>** to find out how many lines are in the editing buffer. Because **^G** (and **:f<CR>**) gives you both of these values in a single response, these alternate commands probably won't get much use. Where the **:.=<CR>** command comes in handy is in supplying line number references to extended editing commands that are issued on the **ex** command line and in the line-editing mode. Their uses will be described in greater detail in Lesson 10.

——— *9.3 Case Conversions* ———

Recent versions of vi have features not found on earlier vintage vi editors, largely because of the increased memory capacities of newer computers and the inevitable evolutionary changes that affect most software over time (often referred to as "creeping featurism"). Here is one such feature.

Convert character case (˜)

The case-conversion feature uses the transliterate operator, a tilde (˜), to translate the character at the cursor to the opposite case and then move the cursor one position to the right. Repetition is achieved by holding down the tilde key on terminals with auto-repeat capability. Some terminals require that a separate *repeat* key be held down simultaneously. Nonalphabetic characters are unaffected by this command and any preceding count is silently ignored.

To change all the letters of the word "control" in the following line to capital letters, move to the beginning of the word and press the tilde key seven times.

Before:

```
                                              SCREEN DATA
Use the control key to input special codes.
```

After:

```
                                              SCREEN DATA
Use the CONTROL_key to input special codes.
```

The cursor comes to rest on the position following the last translated character.

9.4 Joining Lines

In the process of editing text you will sometimes want to join two or more lines together to form a single longer line; vi provides a simple way to do this.

Join lines (**nJ**)

The join command, when given as a capital J (also **1J** or **2J**), appends the line below the current line to the end of the current line. The cursor may be anywhere in the current line—it does not have to be moved to the end of the line.

vi tries to insert the right number of spaces at the place where the lines are joined, usually one space as a word separator. If the character at the end of the current line terminates a sentence (. or ? or !), vi inserts two spaces. If the result is not exactly what you want, it is easy to change the spacing because vi places the cursor in the gap between the two joined lines. Usually typing **x** to delete the offending extra space is all that is required. If the first character of a line being appended to the one before is a (, vi adds no extra space.

If an optional count, *n*, of three or greater is specified, vi attempts to join *n* lines together. If fewer than *n* lines are found from the current line to the end of the editing buffer, vi joins all lines found. In multiline joins, the cursor lands at the juncture of the first two line segments.

To join three short lines into one long line, move to any position in the first line and type **3J**.

Before:

SCREEN DATA

```
Going once,
going twice.
Three times.
Sold!
```

After:

```
                                                                    SCREEN DATA

Going once,__going twice. Three times.
Sold!
```

Note that a single space is inserted at the first juncture because the first line ends with a comma; whereas, two spaces are inserted at the second juncture because the second line of the original text ended in a period.

—— *9.5 Transposing Characters* ——

Probably the most common typographical error is reversing the order of two adjacent characters. Using two simple commands described earlier in succession corrects such an error easily.

Transpose characters (**xp, Xp**)

The **x** deletes the character at the cursor position. The remainder of the line closes up, bringing the character that was just to the right of the cursor under it. The **p** puts back the last deletion after the current cursor position. The effect of the two commands is a transposition of the character at the cursor and the one immediately to its right. The resting place of the cursor after this operation is on the second of the transposed letters. This command sequence cannot be undone by the **u** command because **u** only reverses the effect of the most recent command, in this case the **p** operation.

Before:

```
                                                                    SCREEN DATA

It is easy to tranpsose two letters.
```

After transposition:

```
                                                                    SCREEN DATA
It is easy to transpose two letters.
```

After attempted undo:

```
                                                                    SCREEN DATA
It is easy to transose two letters.
```

If, instead, the cursor is placed on the rightmost of the characters to be transposed and **Xp** is used, the whole operation is reversible by simply typing **Xp** again. This result occurs because **X** deletes the character just to the left of the cursor and moves the remainder of the line left one position. The **p** puts the deleted character to the right of the cursor, which leaves the cursor at its original position in the line, and the two letters of interest are transposed.

9.6 *Shifting Objects*

Now we will "shift" into high gear and talk about more ways to move large amounts of text around in the editing buffer.

```
Shift text objects (n<OBJ, n<<, n>OBJ, n>>)
```

These rather arcane looking commands can be very useful in some circumstances. In text preparation, they make it possible to indent blocks of text evenly and quickly. They are useful to programmers writing block-structured source code where the level of indentation of lines is significant, at least visually.

The amount of indentation (or "undentation" in the case of left shifts) is by the **shiftwidth** variable. The value is often set to three or four columns for programming applications. The default value is eight columns, just like **tabstop**.

To indent a block of four lines starting at the current line type **4>>**. If one level of indentation of these lines is not enough, use the dot command (.) to repeat the effect as many times as necessary to achieve the needed indentation of the block. Removing indentation is just as easy. Type **4<<** to shift the lines to the left by one shiftwidth.

Before shifting:

```
                                                           SCREEN DATA
Here are a few lines of text that
are to be shifted right as a block.
A simple command does the job and
the dot command repeats the effect.
```

After shifting once (shiftwidth = 5):

```
                                                           SCREEN DATA
    Here are a few lines of text that
    are to be shifted right as a block.
    A simple command does the job and
    the dot command repeats the effect.
```

Objects other than whole lines may be specified, but the command always affects whole lines from the current line to the line containing the specified object or screen position. If you need to shift everything from the current line to the end of the buffer to the right by one shiftwidth, type **>G**. Shifting two paragraphs is done by putting the cursor on the first line of the first paragraph and typing **2>}** (or **>2}**). The same can be done for sentences, sections, screen positions (**H, M,** and **L**), and other objects known to **vi**.

To illustrate, use the previous example, but select a range of lines to shift by specifying different text objects. First, to shift lines from the current line to the first one containing the word "right", type **>/right<CR>**.

Before shifting:

```
                                                          SCREEN DATA
Here are a few lines of text that
are to be shifted right as a block.
A simple command does the job and
the dot command repeats the effect.
```

After shifting once (shiftwidth = 5):

```
                                                          SCREEN DATA
     Here are a few lines of text that
     are to be shifted right as a block.
     A simple command does the job and
     the dot command repeats the effect.
```

Undo the change (**u**) and now type **/effect<CR>** to move the cursor to the last line of the example. Use the command **>(** to shift the second sentence to the right by a shiftwidth and then **<)** to restore it to the original position. Experiment with other objects to get a feel for these useful shift commands.

─────────────────── Exercises ───────────────────

1. Invoke **vi** with a file name of an existing text file and make a few cosmetic changes to the editing buffer. Then change the name of a file to "pumpkin". Observe what **vi** tells you about the new file's condition. Repeat this exercise, but this time make no changes to the buffer before renaming the file. What is different?

2. Turn line numbering on if it is off. If there are no long lines in the file you are editing create one by joining two or more short lines and notice how a long line wraps back to the left side when the right edge of the screen is reached. What commands did you use to join the lines? How do you now split the long line into two approximately equal segments?

3. Select any word in the current editing buffer and translate all the letters in it to the opposite case. How can you undo the "damage" you've done?

4. Transpose any two adjacent characters in the file. Try to undo the change. What commands did you use? Try using the other method of transposing characters described in this lesson. Can the change be undone easily?

5. Shift every line in the current editing buffer to the right by one shiftwidth. What is the easiest way to shift them all again by the same amount? Shift all lines back to their original positions. List the commands you used to do these tasks.

LESSON 10 | Using Other Editing Modes

Goals

—Access line-editing mode from visual mode (and return)

—Access open mode from line-editing mode to use visual editing features in a one-line editing window

—Use line-oriented editing features of ex from any of the editor modes

10.1 The ex Editor

The assumption made so far in these lessons is that the visual mode of the ex/vi editor provides nearly all the capability you will need for a wide range of editing tasks. Although this is a good assumption, tasks and situations occur for which the line-editing and open modes are better choices. One example is global search and replace operations. Another example is the use of a low-speed communication line and a dumb terminal, such that vi's constant rewriting of the screen is too time consuming.

Switch to line-editing mode (**Q**)

To leave the visual mode and continue editing the same file in line-editing mode, type **Q** (some early versions of v i used **q** for this purpose). The editor is put into the line-editing mode and the current line remains the same. All editing is done on a one-line-at-a-time basis. All of the operations supported by the standard UNIX line editor, ed, are available, in addition to some new line-oriented capabilities. A little later in this lesson, we'll take a closer look at the line-editing mode.

Switch to visual mode from ex (**vi<CR>**)

To switch back to visual command mode, type **vi<CR>** at the ex prompt (:). The editor will open a window on the editing buffer for the current file with the current line at the top. Use the command variations **vi.<CR>** and **vi-<CR>** to place the current line in the middle and at the bottom of the display window, respectively.

───── 10.2 Invoking the ex Editor ─────

The ex editor may also be started up from the UNIX command line in a way that is analogous to what you have learned about starting v i.

Starting ex (**ex [*option...*] [+*command*] [*file...*]<CR>**)

---

ex takes several options that alter its behavior and control its entry point in the editing buffer. These options and their effects are shown in Table 10-1.

In addition to these options, ex accepts an optional command to set the current line before editing begins. The **command** argument to the + option can be one of the following:

Argument	Description
(none)	Places the cursor at the beginning of the last line in the editing buffer. This is the default for **ex**.
number	Places the cursor at the beginning of line *number*.
/*str*<*CR*>	Places the cursor at the beginning of the first line that contains the string *str*. If *str* is not found, the last line is used as if no positioning command had been given.

A file name or list of file names may be specified on the ex invocation command line. The names of these files, if any, are retained in the argument list, which may be viewed (**args**), traversed with the **n** command, and rewound to the first entry (**rewind**).

Table 10-1. Command-line Options for ex

Option	Description
-	Silences ex. All user feedback messages are turned off, thus permitting the use of ex editor scripts (files that contain editing commands).
-v	Starts the editor in the visual mode. This has the same effect as invoking vi directly.
-t*tag*	Causes ex to obtain the starting file and position information from the tags file entry called *tag*.
-r	Recovers files saved by ex (or vi) when an interrupt or system crash occurred. If no file names are given on the command line, this option displays a list of saved files.
-l	Sets the **lisp** and **showmatch** variables to enable Lisp program editing.
-w*n*	Sets the initial display window size to n lines.

——— *10.3 Open Editing Mode* ———

Open mode is a special one-line window version of the vi mode of the editor. It may be accessed only from the line-editing mode. Also, if you start up vi running a dumb or an unknown terminal type, the editor will switch to open mode and issue a warning message:

[Unknown terminal type. Using open mode]

Open mode is recommended when you want to use vi editing commands on a terminal of dubious intellect. It is also useful with connections over a slow communication channel. Open mode editing can be done on printing terminals, too, thus extending vi capabilities in a modified form to virtually all terminals.

Switch to open mode (**open<CR>**)

From the line-editing command mode prompt, type **open<CR>** to access open mode. In open mode, nearly all vi commands and features are available to you.

The major limitation of open mode is that all text is displayed in a one-line window. When text is scrolled in either direction, each new line is displayed below the last displayed line, which is a bit confusing to new users at first. Turning on the line-numbering option helps quite a bit (**set nu<CR>**).

The only two vi commands that work differently in open mode are **z** and **^R**. The use of **z** is limited to redrawing a window of context around the current line and then redisplaying the current line for editing. With a window size of eight lines, the cursor at the start of the word "justice" in the "US__Cons" file, and line numbering set on, the **z** command results in this display appearance.

After a **z** command in open mode:

```
                                                              SCREEN DATA

2   the people of the United States,
3   in order to form a more perfect Union,
----------------------------------------
4   establish justice,
----------------------------------------
5   insure domestic tranquility,
6   provide for the common defense,


4   establish _justice,
```

The current line is shown between the dashed lines and within the context of the surrounding lines. It also appears one line below the displayed block. This location is where the open mode editing is done. On video terminals only one copy of the line is displayed. On hard-copy terminals, there are two copies on adjacent lines. The top line is what the line looked like before editing, and the second line is where changes are reflected.

The refresh command, **^R**, redisplays the current line and shows its most recent condition. On hard-copy terminals using a two-line presentation as described in the previous paragraph, **^R** shows the line in both its unedited and edited forms.

Leave the open mode in exactly the same way that you leave visual mode. Simply type **Q**. Also, all of the same file handling commands and options are available, and argument lists are supported in open mode.

— 10.4 Line-Oriented Editing with ex —

The same editor start-up file (.exrc) or shell variable (EXINIT) used to customize vi will initialize ex. Variables that have no purpose in line-editing mode are ignored.

The ex prompt is a colon (:), which is an invitation for you to type a command. All ex commands have a common form, with all parts except the terminating **<CR>** being optional. A lone **<CR>** makes the next line in the editing buffer current and displays it.

The general form of line-editing mode commands is

[address][command][!]*[parameters][count][flags]*<CR>

Each of the parts is described here.

address: Addresses are formed from a set of address primitives summarized in Table 10-2. The primitives are used singly or in pairs separated by a comma for most commands. These are called address expressions. Addresses may be "stacked" by using a semicolon between individual address expressions. The expressions are evaluated left to right, and the value of the current line (.) in an expression is its value after any preceding address expression is evaluated.

command:	Many of the commands you have learned and used with vi are applicable to ex. A summary of ex commands is presented in the following list. For harmony with the vi editor mode, ex ignores a leading : if one is typed as part of a command string.
!:	Invokes a variant form of the ***command***. Many of the commands have two distinct types of behavior. Often this means that some editor variable is modified. For example, the setting of the **autoindent** variable.
parameters:	A parameter modifies and controls the behavior of the ***command*** in some way. A parameter is usually a file name, a command option, or a variable name.
count:	Supplies a repetition factor to some commands.
flags:	These are signals to the editor that the command should act globally within a line (**g**), display all affected lines (**p**), and display tab and newline characters (**l**).

Line addresses and text used in search strings may be specified by using regular expressions. A regular expression specifies a set of character strings rather than simple literal character strings. Appendix D describes regular expressions and their uses.

Virtually all of the commands in vi introduced by a leading colon (:) are line-editing mode commands, so you already know a lot about line-editing mode. The commands include the read (**r<CR>**), write (**w<CR>**), edit (**e<CR>**), quit (**q<CR>**), and line positioning (*n*<CR>) commands, the **args<CR>**, **rew<CR>**, and n<CR> commands for managing the argument list, and **set** *OPT*<CR> for viewing and controlling editor variables.

The append, change, delete, and insert commands have direct analogs in ex, also. You can use **file<CR>** to get a status report or to change the current file name. In addition, line-editing mode offers a few more commands and adds a few twists to some others that are available in the visual mode.

Table 10-2. Addressing Primitives.

Address Primitive	Description
. (dot)	The current line, which is usually set to the last line affected by an ex command, and initially to the last line in the editing buffer when ex reads in a new file.
n	Lines in the buffer are numbered starting at 1, so *n* is the *n*th line.
$	The last line in the editing buffer, which is the position ex seeks when it first reads in a file unless this is changed using a + (positioning) command.
%	This is a shorthand notation for the address range 1,$, which means the entire editing buffer.
+*n* -*n*	These values provide offsets from the current line (.)
/*pat* ?*pat*?/	These search forward (/) or backward (?) in the editing buffer for *pat*, wrapping around the beginning or end of the editing buffer. The search string, *pat*, is a regular expression. Empty or null search strings assume the value of the previously specified regular expression, if any. Either form used with or without a trailing / or ? displays the matched line, which becomes the current line.
' '	(2 single quotes) Returns to the line of the previous editing context following most positioning commands.
'*x*	Returns to the line explicitly identified by the mark *x*.

Append text (***addr*append<CR>**)

The **append** command (**a** for brevity) adds text to the buffer after the current line by default or after line ***addr*** if one is specified. Input is terminated with a dot (.) on a line by itself. An address of 0 is valid with this command. Text is appended at the beginning of the buffer.

If the command is followed by an exclamation point (**a!**), the **autoindent** variable is reversed only during the current text insertion. Therefore, if **noai** is the current setting, the automatic indentation feature will be enabled temporarily.

Change text (***addr1,addr2*change *count***)

Text in the range of lines from ***addr1*** to ***addr2*** (the default is the current line) is replaced by new text. If ***count*** is specified, then the text replacement is made for ***count*** lines beginning with the current line. Text insertion is terminated by a dot (.) on a line by itself. As with the **append** command, a trailing **!** toggles the **autoindent** variable for the duration of the insert operation.

Copy lines (***addr1,addr2*copy *addr3 flags*<CR>**)

A copy of the specified lines is added to the buffer after the line specified by ***addr3***. The current line is set to the last of the lines in the copy. The command may be abbreviated to **co** or **t**.

Delete lines (***addr1,addr2*delete *buffer count flags*<CR>**)

The **delete** command (or simply **d**) removes the specified lines from the editing buffer. If a named ***buffer*** (a-z) is specified, it saves the deleted lines. Using an uppercase name for ***buffer*** (A-Z) causes lines to be appended to the contents of **buffer**. A **count** may be used in lieu of line addresses, in which case **count** lines starting with the current line are deleted. The line following the deleted lines becomes the new current line.

Global (**addr1,addr2global /pattern/commands**<CR>

The **global** command makes two passes through the specified range of lines in the editing buffer, first to mark lines that contain a match to **pattern**, and then to execute the command list given by **commands** on each of the matching lines. If an address range is not specified, the entire buffer is assumed.

The types of commands that may be used in the command list range from simple text replacements to very sophisticated editing tasks using append, insert, and change commands. Even open or visual mode editing commands are permitted—input is taken from the terminal in such cases.

The variant **g!/pattern/commands** runs **commands** on each line in the editing buffer that does not match **pattern**.

Insert text (**addr**insert<CR>

The **insert** command (**i** for short) adds text to the editing buffer before the line specified by **addr** (the current line is the default). Text insertion mode is terminated by a dot (.) on a line by itself.

The command variant **i!** toggles the **autoindent** for the duration of the insert operation.

List lines (**addr1,addr2**list **count**<CR>)

The list command prints lines from the buffer by using printing symbols for characters otherwise not visible on a terminal screen. Tabs are displayed as ^I, and the end-of-line marker is displayed as

$. When the listing is complete, the last line displayed becomes the current line.

Either line addresses or a count of lines may be specified to tell **list** what lines to display. (If both are specified, the addresses are overridden by the count.) The default is to display only the current line.

This command shows whether tabs or spaces are responsible for blank areas in displayed text, and it clearly shows up any trailing whitespace at the ends of lines. In other respects, it is identical to **print**. If the editor variable **list** is set, then this is the default mode of line display.

Mark buffer (***addr*mark** *x***<CR>**)

Mark buffer (***addr*k*x***<CR>**)

The **mark** command parallels the one command in **vi** except that it has no abbreviation (**m** means **move** to **ex**) and there must be whitespace between the command name and the character that identifies the mark. For convenience, a synonym, **k**, may be used. It does not need whitespace between the command name and the mark identifier. If ***addr*** is specified, the addressed line is marked. The current line (.) is the default.

A line marked by the command **mark a<CR>** is addressed by using the command '**a**. Because **ex** works on whole lines, there is no equivalent to the **vi** command `x to move to some interior portion of a marked line.

Move lines (***addr1,addr2*m*addr3*<CR>**)

The move command deletes lines ***addr1*** through ***addr2*** and puts them back in the buffer after line ***addr3***. Line ***addr1***, at its new position, becomes the current line. Empty line addresses for the "from" lines are assumed to be the line that is current before the command executes. Thus **m10<CR>** moves the current line to the line after line 10 and pushes the following lines further down in the buffer.

Display text lines (***addr1,addr2*print** *count***<CR>**)

This command may be abbreviated to **p** or **P**. It displays text lines in the range ***addr1*** to ***addr2*** in an unambiguous way by converting nonprinting characters to their control character representations. An embedded backspace prints as ^H, a delete character as ^?, and so on. Tabs and spaces are displayed as blanks unless the **list** editor variable is set.

Either line addresses or a count of lines may be specified to tell **print** what lines to display. (If both are specified, the addresses are overridden by the count.) The default is to display only the current line.

A variation of this command substitutes the name **number** for **print**. The abbreviations **nu** and **#** may be used. It behaves identically to **print** except that all displayed lines are preceded by a line number.

Search (**/***text***/+*n***<CR>** or **?***text***?+*n***<CR>**)

I mentioned the search capability in an earlier lesson, but I only touched upon a few of its capabilities. The **/** (forward slash) looks for a string matching ***text*** from the cursor toward the end of the editing buffer and the **?** looks backward from the cursor toward the beginning of the buffer.

The search commands identify positions within a line where a pattern match occurs. In line-editing mode, commands to change, delete, substitute, and so on, affect whole lines, not portions of lines. Commands like **d/relative<CR>** where the searched for string is used as a text object do not work predictably from one version of the editor to another.

An optional relative number, shown as ***+n***, may be used to force the match to a whole line, which is important when the search is combined with a **delete** or other command. To force the search to match the line containing the matching text string, use a **+0** following the search string, as in the command

d/relative/+0

The number may also be a nonzero value, either positive or negative to force a match with a line greater than or less than the one containing the matching text.

Run commands from a file (**source** *file*<CR>)

This command, which may be abbreviated to **so**, lets you use editor scripts from a file to automate the process of editing files. The editor script files may include other **source** commands to any depth.

Substitute (*addr1,addr2s/pat/repl/ opts n flgs*<CR>)

The **substitute** command, abbreviated to **s**, deletes the first occurrence of *pat* in lines in the specified range. If the "global" flag is present, all occurrences in any line in the specified range are changed. The last line in which a substitution occurs becomes the current line.

If the "confirm" option is specified, the **substitution** command prompts the user for confirmation before proceeding with the replacement operation. A 'y' response confirms the replacement. Any other key bypasses it.

Undo (**undo**<CR>)

The ex version of undo, abbreviated to **u**, differs from the vi version in a few respects. Any global commands, entire editing sessions in an instance of visual or open mode, and an **undo** itself can be reversed by this command. Commands that interact with the

UNIX file system (such as **write** and **edit**, a simplified version of ex) cannot be reversed.

Version (**ver<CR>**)

You can find out what version of the editor is running on your system by typing **ver<CR>**. The editor displays a brief message that tells you both the version number and date of release of the editor source code to authorized institutions and vendors. But you will usually not be able to tell what enhancements have been made to the editor or what features have been left out by local personnel or by the vendor except by using the editor.

"Zero" display window (*addrz type count*<CR>)

The line-editing mode **z** command is a bit more limited than its visual counterpart. The *type* part of the command tells the editor where to place the addressed line (current line by default) in the display window. **<CR>** puts the line at the top, dot (.) places it at the center, and a dash (-) places it at the bottom of the text display window. If a *count* is specified, it sets a display window size that temporarily overrides the default size.

If a *count* is specified, but not a *type*, the z command displays the number of lines specified by the editor variable **window** beginning with the one specified by *addr* (the one after the current line by default).

—————————————— Exercises ——————————————

1. Assume that you are editing a file with **vi** and suddenly you get an error message, "Internal error" and a colon prompt. What are your options at this point? How can you continue editing in visual mode?

2. If you are editing with vi on a slow, dumb video terminal, how can you get to the open mode from visual mode? Why might you want to do this?

3. From the UNIX command line, how do you edit a file "japan" with the ex editor starting at the first occurrence of "Samurai"? At the last occurrence of the same word?

4. In line-editing mode, how do you move lines 40-60 inclusive to a point in the editing buffer following line 27? (Assume that the current line is 46.) When this operation is completed, what is the editor's notion of the current line?

5. What line-editing command prints an unambiguous listing of lines between the current line and the end of the buffer for all lines that contain the pattern "floppy disk"?

6. Write a line-editing command that replaces all occurrences of the number "3" in the editing buffer with "three". How can you run this command while editing in visual mode without leaving visual mode? How do you restore the original buffer contents after such a change?

Special
Features

Goals

—Use macros to simplify repetitive tasks

—Use abbreviations to reduce data entry effort

—Use tags to simplify and speed access to text blocks

The features described in this lesson apply only to version 3.0 and later ex/vi editors.

—— *11.1 Macros in Command Mode* ——

Just as we use a chart or map to condense information about the real world to convenient, manageable proportions, so too can we shrink relatively large and complex commands and expressions into compact representations, preferably single keystrokes. When it is used by a program, a small item, the "macro" is expanded into its full-sized equivalent.

Define a macro (**:map** *lhs rhs*<**CR**>)

Delete a macro (**:unmap** *lhs*<**CR**>)

The vi and ex editors permit the use of parameterless macros, which are single-purpose macros that can not take any arguments, or parameters, to alter their behavior. Even without support for parameters, vi's macros give you considerable power and flexibility to create your own special command and data entry combinations.

You define macros using the map command. The command has the form :**map** *lhs rhs*<CR>, where *lhs* (left-hand string) is often a single keystroke or a special control code or function key, and *rhs* (right-hand string) is the command sequence you want vi to run. The <CR> terminates the macro definition. If you want a literal carriage return to be emitted as part of the expanded command sequence, it must be quoted using a ^V to distinuish it from the map command terminator.

Here is a simple example of a macro. It condenses an often used command squence, a shell escape, into a control key operation. We will use ^X for the macro name and define it by typing this sequence:

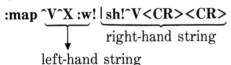

:map ^V^X :w! | sh!^V<CR><CR>

right-hand string

left-hand string

in which the ^V character quotes the character immediately following it, thus allowing the "quoted" character to be part of the macro name or definition instead of having an immediate effect. The command name itself must be quoted because it is a control character. The first carriage return has to be quoted because it is part of the command, but the second carriage return is not quoted because it tells the editor that this is the end of the macro definition. The on-screen appearance of the macro definition is **map ^X :w! | sh^M**, where ^M is the visible symbol used by the editor to display a carriage return.

The | is used to separate commands in a command list that ex will run in sequence. This is not the same as a UNIX shell's pipeline directive—no information is being passed from one command to the next. In fact, it is analogous to the use of a ; (semicolon) to separate UNIX shell commands.

The effect of this macro when you call it by typing ^X is to save the editing buffer to the current file on disk, then run an indefinite subshell. After working in the subshell, you can continue editing by typing a ^D to the subshell, which will return you to v i on the exact line of your previous editing context.

The same capabilities apply to ex and open modes—macros work the same way throughout the editor. For repeated use, macro definitions may be placed in an editor startup file or shell variable to automate the process.

At any time you may delete a macro definition by using the command :**unmap** *lhs*<CR>. This command erases the mapping of the left-hand string to the right-hand string, leaving the original *lhs* free for some other use or allowing space for another macro definition.

Please note a few cautions and limitations. Each system places a limit on how many macros may be defined (check local customs), and there is a maximum length of 10 characters for the *lhs* and 100 characters for the *rhs*. The *lhs* must be short and easy because it has to be typed within one second, hence, the preference for single key macro names. Be sure to select carefully the option to write (or not write) the editing buffer to the associated file—there are times when updating is necessary and others when it is not.

Here is a macro that will find the start of a paragraph and insert a tab ahead of the first character. If there is already some white-space there, it will get some more. The mapping is

  :**map #1 {I^I^VESC<CR>**,

where the ^V is needed to prevent the **ESC** from ending the macro definition prematurely. It must be part of the command to end the insert mode. The #1 macro name is special: It refers to the first of up to 10 function keys on terminals that have them. On those terminals that don't have functions keys, the separate characters # and 1 are pressed to simulate function key one and similarly for others. In such cases, the one-second limitation on typing the *lhs* is waived.

Before:

```
                                            SCREEN DATA

The sound of the thunder crashing along the ridge
was deafening as we clung nervously to the jagged
rocks.
```

After typing function key 1:

```
                                            SCREEN DATA

    The sound of the thunder crashing along the ridge
was deafening as we clung nervously to the jagged
rocks.
```

Another way to use macros depends on having named buffers (sometimes referred to as registers) hold command strings. The technique requires that a named buffer be filled with a command string of no more than 512 characters. The buffer should not be used for any other purpose to preclude loss of the command information.

To load the "x" buffer, for example, type the command on a line by itself and then delete it into the buffer, like so. Type **o** (for a new input line), followed by the command string, and then **ESC**. Assuming the file you are editing contains one or more occurences of the word "the", let's change each of them to "THE", just for show and tell.

The new line containing a command:

```
                                            SCREEN DATA

:g/the/s//THE/g
```

The line is automatically terminated with a newline character by vi. Now delete the line into the "x" buffer by typing **"xdd**. The command and the newline have been saved in the "x" buffer.

To use the saved command, type **@x** and watch the results. The macro, in this case the "at sign" followed by the buffer name, is expanded by v i to the command stored in the buffer, so the effect is identical to typing **:g/the/s//THE/g<CR>**. Because it is a single command to v i, its effect can be reversed with a single undo command. Type @ @ to repeat the most recent macro call.

11.2   Abbreviations and Mapped
Strings

Repetitive tasks occur during text input operations, too. The editor offers two methods of permitting abbreviated text input.

Define an abbreviation (**:abbr** *str1 str2*)

Define a character mapping (**:map!** *str1 str2*)

Defining abbreviations is done with either of the commands just shown—their results are virtually identical. To avoid typing a frequently used phrase or name, you can create a short, unique name that gets expanded upon input. Thus, the name of a fictional company, Pucilanimous Instrument Company, could be abbreviated to "pic" by typing **:abbr pic Pucilanimous Instrument Company<CR>**. The **<CR>** ends the abbreviation command; it is not part of the expanded string.

As you type new input, v i detects *str1*, pic, and upon receiving the next character, it replaces *str1* with its definition, *str2*.

Str1 is typed:

SCREEN DATA

```
Our market share has steadily declined in recent years.
The market for pic__
```

After a trailing character (space) is typed:

```
                                                    SCREEN DATA
Our market share has steadily declined in recent years.
The market for Pucilanimous Instrument Company __
```

The **:map!** form could be used to "map" *str1* into *str2* to achieve the same result. Experience, most of it bad, has shown that this is not yet a reliable feature. Use **abbreviate** instead.

11.3 Tags and Tag Files

Both programmers and documentors can benefit from the tags feature of vi. It is a feature that permits quick access to known parts of source and document files.

Edit tagged item (**:ta** *label*)

Create a tags file (**ctags** *[options] file...*)

Tags are symbolic references to items in much the same way that your address is a symbolic reference to where you live. Tags provide a quick and easy way to locate a program function in a set of source files or an important item in a set of document files, provided that they are all in one directory. The references are prepared and stored in a file called "tags", which is a simple-minded data base. Each record or line in a tags file contains three items separated by whitespace, usually a tab; a label, a file name, and a search string.

You can manually create a tags file by using the editor of your choice as long as it produces simple ASCII character files. For C language programs, a utility program named **ctags** automatically creates a tags file for all functions in one or more source files (all .h and .c files) in a single directory.

NOTE:

The **ctags** program was developed at the University of California at Berkeley. It is available on many UNIX systems but may not be offered on your system. It is available on some systems as nonsupported software.

Using a document example first, a tags file might contain references to the major topics, key discussion points, or whatever you are likely to deal with regularly. The labels must be sorted, and each must be unique.

If you are editing a file and the buffer has been modified, write or abandon the changes before calling on the tags feature. If you forget and type **:ta** and a label, vi will bark at you and display the message *No write since last change*. Write or abandon the file, then type **:ta<CR>**, and vi will use the label it remembered from your previous attempt.

Managing the files used in the preparation of the manuscript for this book is a good example of tags in action. A partial display of the tags file looks like this:

```
                                                          SCREEN DATA
$ cat tags
append    lsn03.n  ?vi   Insert Mode?
delete    lsn04.n  ?Deleting Text?
.
.
.
repeat    lsn04.n  ?Repeating Commands?
starting  lsn01.n  ?Getting Started?
setup     lsn01.n  ?Initial Setup?
```

You can invoke the editor by using a UNIX command line such as **vi -t starting<CR>**, for example, to begin editing the section on starting the editor. The editor reads in the file "lsn01.n" and searches for the string "Getting Started". If you specify a tag that does not exist, say "zulu", the editor opens an empty editing buffer and displays a message:

zulu: No such tag in tags file

Programmers get a lot of help from the ctags program. Using ctags is easy. Just give it the names of the files you want included in the tags file and it generates the data base entries and sorts them by label names, which are generally the names of all functions in all named files. The files must all be in the same directory, and the resultant tags file will reside there, too.

Only the main function is given special treatment to permit tags to work in directories that contain more than one complete program. For each main( ) found, the name of the file it is contained in is prefixed with a letter M, and its .c extension is lopped off. If a function other than main( ) appears in more than one of the files, a warning message is issued by ctags, and only one reference is placed in the data base.

Let's assume we have a directory that contains sorting programs that are under development. Two of the files are "driver" programs and several other files contain sorting functions, one per file.

File name	Function in the file
sds.c	main( )
sdx.c	main( )
shell.c	shell( )
shell2.c	shell( )
xsort.c	xsort( )

Running the ctags program produces a warning message and a tags file.

```
                                                        SCREEN DATA
$ ctags *
Duplicate function in files shell2.c and shell.c: shell
(Warning only)''
$ cat tags
Msds   sds.c     ?^main(argc, argv )$?
Msdx   sdx.c     ?^main(argc, argv)$?
shell  shell.c   ?^shell(a, n)$?
xsort  xsort.c   ?^xsort(a, n)$?
```

To move the editing context to the main function in the file sds.c, type **:ta Msds<CR>** and wait while vi loads the file and moves to the main function. Later, you can type **:ta shell<CR>** to edit the shell sorting function.

─────────────────────── Exercises ───────────────────────

NOTE: These exercises can be done only on systems that are running vi, version 3.0 or later. The ctags program must be available if you want to try Exercise 6.

1. Define macro in your own words. Why are macros useful?

2. Write a command macro that, when invoked, finds the next occurrence of a blank line in the editing buffer.

3. Using a named buffer, write and use a macro that inserts a plus sign at the end of the current line. Use the buffer "e" (for end) and invoke it as @e. Move onto other lines and rerun the command by using the @@ command.

4. Create an abbreviation for your full name and then use the abbreviated form in some input to see the effect. Do the same thing using the character mapping method. Do you notice any difference between the methods?

5. Create a tags file for the "usc" document file that has tags for the first occurrence of "United States", "Union", and "Constitution". Use the tags option from the UNIX command line to edit the file at the specified position by using the tags file you just created.

6. If you are a programmer and have a C program in a directory that currently has no tags file, use ctags to create one. View the resultant "tags" file and use it with vi to edit one of the tagged items. Then use it from within the editor to switch to another tagged item.

Command
Reference

This section contains an ordered set of manual pages for the primary vi and ex commands and operators. Each page lists the name of the command or operator, its syntax, and a functional description. In addition, a brief example of its use is provided.

Below the title on each page is a reference to the section number in which a detailed tutorial description of the command or operator is presented in this book.

ABBREVIATE

(11.2)

Name

abbreviate—define an abbreviation for a text sequence

Syntax

:abbr *str1 str2*<CR>

Description

Abbreviations give you a shorthand means of inputting complicated and often-used text sequences. The command **abbr** (or simply **ab**) takes two string arguments, *str1,* the abbreviation you wish to use, and *str2,* the expanded string that is placed in the editing buffer.

The abbreviation should not be a word that you will want to input literally, such as "art" or "dad." The abbreviation will not be expanded if it is keyed in as part of a larger string—only when it stands alone, surrounded by whitespace (blank, tab, or newline).

Example

:abbr ic intergrated circuit<CR>—create an abbreviation for "integrated circuit" called "ic".

── *ALTERNATE FILE* ──

(7.4)

Name

#—the remembered name of the alternate file

Syntax

#

Description

The vi/ex editor remembers the names of two files (and their associated editing bufers)—the "current" and the "alternate" file. The alternate file is the file not visible on the screen.

Example

Look for the phrase "something special" in the alternate file without leaving the editor.

```
:grep ''something special'' #<CR>
```

APPEND

(3.3)

Name

a, A—append text to the editing buffer

Syntax

*a*textESC or *A*textESC

Description

The append operators accept text until the escape character (ESC) is typed. The **a** operator appends text to the right of the cursor and pushes existing text further to the right.

The **A** operator moves the cursor to the end of the line and then appends new text to it. Any amount of text may be appended, but the wrapmargin feature may be fooled under some conditions.

Example

Append some text to the end of the current line.

A And that's final!ESC

ARGS

(7.6)

Name

args—list of remembered file names

Syntax

:args<CR>

Description

The editor retains a list of file names in an "argument list" that may be viewed by typing **:args<CR>**. The files may be given to v i at the time the editor is started by using arguments on the command line or while within the editor by using the **:n** *file...*<CR> command.

You may move to the next file in the list by typing **:n<CR>** and to the beginning of the list by typing **:rewind<CR>**.

Example

Enter a new file list without leaving the editor.

`:n file?.c framus.c xfile.pas<CR>.`

BUFFER

(4.6)

Name

%, #, a-z, 1-9, unnamed—main and auxiliary text buffers

Syntax

%, #, a, 1

Description

The editor maintains many buffers for text. The current buffer (%) and the alternate buffer (#) are the primary text storage areas; each holds the contents of an entire file. In addition, there are numbered (1-9) and named (a-z) buffers, and one unnamed buffer.

The numbered buffers collect text in whole lines from operations that delete text from the current editing buffer. The named buffers may be used to collect text on demand, and they are frequently used to move blocks of text from one editing buffer to another.

Example

' '2p

CHANGE

(4.3)

Name

c, C—change text beginning at the cursor position.

Syntax

c*OBJtext*ESC or **C*text*ESC**

Description

The change operators accept text until you type an escape (**ESC**) character. Text may include control characters if they are quoted with ^**V** to make them visible. The c version of the operator replaces text from the cursor position to the specified object (**w, e,), }, /*text*,** and so on) with any amount of new text.

C is a synonym for **c$,** which replaces text from the cursor to the end of the line with new text.

Example

Change the current word to "replacement words".

```
cwreplacement wordsESC
```

— *CONVERT* —

(9.3)

Name

~—convert the character at the cursor to the opposite case

Syntax

~

Description

The ~ operator converts a lowercase letter to uppercase or an uppercase letter to lowercase. Nonalphabetic characters are not affected. Only the character at the cursor position is affected. The cursor moves to the right one position after each attempt at a conversion.

CURSOR

(2.1)

Name

h, j, k, l—move the cursor left, down, up, and right

Syntax

n, *n*j, *n*k, *n*l

Description

The **h** and **l** commands move the cursor one column position left and right, respectively. A count, *n*, can be given to multiply the effect. Thus, **10h** moves the cursor 10 columns to the left, but not past the line boundary.

Similarly, **j** and **k** move the cursor down and up a line, respectively, or *n* lines if a count is given. The screen will scroll if necessary to keep the cursor in view.

Example

5k—move up five lines

DELETE

(4.2)

Name

d, D—delete text from the editing buffer

Syntax

nd*OBJ* or **d**n*OBJ*

Description

The delete operator may be combined with various objects and optional counts to delete text from the editing buffer. Objects in delete commands are typically words (**dw**), sentences (**d)**), and positions (**dL, dG,** and **d$**). The **d$** may be abbreviated to **D,** and doubling the operator name as usual operates on whole lines (**dd**).

You may use search (**/, ?**), find (**f, F**), and move-to (**t,T**) operators to define objects for deletion.

Example

Delete from the cursor up to but not including the string "last word".

d/last word<CR>

ESCAPE

(3.3)

Name

ESC—the escape character terminates input and some commands

Syntax

ESC

Description

The **ESC** character is used to terminate keyboard input and may be used to execute some commands. Commands that cause text to be inserted into the buffer (except **r,** which is self completing) require an **ESC** to tell vi to return to the command mode.

ex editor commands (prefixed by :) may be executed with a trailing **ESC.** However, **<CR>** is a better choice for command termination because it is consistent with the method used in line-editing mode where **ESC** is not an acceptable terminator.

Example

The **ESC** ends the test append operation.

aThe line has been extended.ESC

FILE

(9.1)

Name

:file—associate a file name with the current editing buffer

Syntax

:file *filename*<CR>

Description

The command name may be abbreviated to **f**. When used alone, **file** delivers a summary of information about the current editing buffer contents (name, size, position of the current line in the editing buffer).

When *filename* is specified, the **file** command associates the contents of the editing buffer with *filename,* forgetting any previous association.

Example

Associate a new file name with the current editing buffer.

```
:f newfile<CR>
```

——— *FILTER* ———

(8.4)

Name

!—filter a portion of the editing buffer

Syntax

!OBJcmd<CR>

Description

The filtering capability of the visual mode may be used to modify portions of the editing buffer with commands (UNIX filters) external to the editor. *OBJ* may be any object known to the editor, although things like paragraphs and sections work best. The lines in the specified range in the buffer become input to the external filter command, and the output of the filter program replaces the original input.

The effect of a filtering operation can be reversed by undo.

Example

Convert the lines up to the next paragraph indicator or blank line to a two-column listing.

!}pr -t2<CR>

FIND

(2.3)

Name

f, F—find a character in the current line

Syntax

n*f***c** or **n***F***c**

Description

Find the *n*th occurrence of the character *c* and place the cursor on it. If the character is not found in the current line, the editor beeps and does not move the cursor.

The **f** form seeks the specified character in the forward direction (toward the end) in the buffer. **F** searches in the backward direction. Use the ; (semicolon) to repeat the find operation in the same direction and the , (comma) to repeat the operation in the reverse direction. The find operators may form objects for other editing operators such as delete, change, and yank.

Example

Find the next occurrence of a dash (-) to the right in the current text line.

f -

GLOBAL

(10.4)

Name

g—run an editing command having global effect

Syntax

:addr1,addr2g/str/cmd<CR>

Description

The global command contruct is taken from the line-oriented portion of the vi/ex editor. The global command operates on lines from **addr1** to **addr2** (the whole buffer by default) and executes the command **cmd** for all lines matching the global search string, **str.**

The search string of such commands may contain regular expressions. The addresses may be absolute (a literal line number) or relative values (**.+3**, **/str**, and so on).

Example

Do a global search for lines that contain the string "help" at the beginning and translate each occurrence to "HELP".

```
:g/^help/s//HELP/<CR>
```

GOTO

(2.4)

Name

G—go to a specified line in the editing buffer

Syntax

nG

Description

The "goto" operator moves the cursor to the beginning of the specified line, n, if it is within the range of lines in the buffer. If n is not specified, the G operator moves the cursor to the last line of the buffer.

G used as an object to another operator marks the end of the editing buffer; thus, the command dG deletes the current line and all remaining lines in the buffer.

Example

Delete from the current line up to and including what is now line number 21.

d21G

INSERT

(3.3)

Name

i, I—insert text in the editing buffer

Syntax

i*text***ESC** or **I***text***ESC**

Description

The insert operators accept text until you type an escape character. Text may include control characters if they are quoted with ^V to make them visible. The **i** version of the operator puts new text in the editing buffer at the cursor position and pushes existing text to the right.

The **I** version inserts text starting at the first nonblank position in the current line. It does the same job as typing ↑ to move to the start of the line and then **i** to insert.

Example

Insert the string "This is some new material." at the current position.

iThis is some new material.ESC

JOIN

(9.4)

Name

J—join two or more lines into a single line

Syntax

nJ

Description

The join operator patches short line segments into one longer line. The optional count, **n**, tells vi how many lines to join. The cursor may be anywhere in the first of the lines to be joined.

The editor tries to put the right number of spaces at the juncture of the line segments on the basis of the punctuation and context. If extra space is put in, use **x** to delete it. If not enough space is inserted to suit you, use the **i** operator to add some.

Example

4J—joins the current line and the following three together as a single line.

MAP

Name

map, unmap, map!—create or delete a macro

Syntax

:map *lhs rhs*<CR>

:unmap *lhs*<CR>

:map! *str1 str2*<CR>

Description

A macro, in simple terms, is something small that stands for something larger and usually more complex. The editor **map** command internally converts a left-hand string (*lhs*) to a right-hand string (*rhs*). You can tell the editor to forget a previously defined macro by using the **unmap** command. A variant of the **map** command, **map**, works like the abbreviate command, which defines a string replacement that is executed during insert mode.

Example

Define a mapping of ^P to a command that sends a formatted listing of the current file (the disk resident file) to the line printer.

```
:map ^P :!pr % | lpr&^M
```

MARK

(2.6, 10.4)

Name

m—place an invisible mark in the editing buffer

Syntax

mx

Description

The name of the mark, **x**, may be any lowercase letter. The mark operator places an invisible mark in the editing buffer that may be used as an object to other v i operators, including "move to" ('**x** *and* `**x**), change (**c'x**), delete (**d'x**), and so on. The mark remains in the editing buffer until it is reused, or until the marked position is deleted, or until the editing session is terminated.

The editor creates additional marks called ' and ` that are automatically placed in the buffer when you make some moves like a search, a "goto" line, or a "move-to" mark operation. Return to these marks by doubling the operator name. ' ' moves the cursor to the beginning of the line containing the mark and `` to the exact position of the mark in the line.

Example

ma—place the invisible mark, **a**, at the current position.

MOVETO

(2.3)

Name

t, T—move cursor next to a specified character

Syntax

ntc or *nTc*

Description

The "moveto" operator moves the cursor right (t) or left (**T**) to a position just before the specified character, *c*. If a count *n* is given, the effect is multiplied, hence **2Tx** moves to the position just to the right of the second x looking backward in the buffer. Use the semicolon (;) to repeat the find operation in the same direction and the comma (,) to repeat in the reverse direction.

The moveto operator may form an object used by delete, change, yank, and other operators.

Example

Delete up to but not including the next occurrence of the letter g.

dtg

OPEN

(3.3)

Name

o, O—open a line for input below or above the current line

Syntax

o or **O**

Description

To open a line below the current line, type **o** and then the text you want to place in the buffer. Terminate the input with an **ESC**. You may place text in the editing buffer above the current line by using the **O** operator.

Example

Open a new line below the current line for input

o

OVERTYPE

(4.3)

Name

R—replace (overtype) text until an ESC is typed

Syntax

R*text*ESC

Description

The **R** operator causes existing text to be replaced starting at the cursor position and proceeding to the right for each character typed. An **ESC** terminates the replacement.

The replacement becomes a straight insertion operation if you continue typing past the end of the existing line.

Example

```
Rreplacement textESC
```

PRESERVE

(6.4)

Name

:preserve—simulate a crash to preserve the buffer contents

Syntax

:preserve\<CR\>

Description

If the write command produces an error and you cannot save your work in any other way, use the **preserve** command to write a copy of the editing buffer to a temporary system directory. The file should be recovered as quickly as possible to avoid unintentional loss. See someone who is responsible (system administrator, for example) for your system as soon as you can to find out what went wrong and correct the problem.

If you are the administrator, look for problems caused by a user logged onto a read-only file system or working in a nonwriteable directory.

Example

Preserves the current buffer contents for later recovery.

:preserve\<CR\>

PUT

(4.4, 10.4)

Name

p, P—put text from a buffer into the main editing buffer

Syntax

np or **nP** or **"xp** or **"xP**

Description

Use the put operators to retrieve text from temporary buffers, text which may be saved from earlier deletes, changes, and yanks. The **p** form puts text to the right of the cursor position, and the **P** form puts the text to the left of it. The forms that have a preceding count, **n** (the default is one), retrieve the specified number of copies of the unnamed buffer's contents. The forms that begin with a double quote retrieve text from named (a-z) and numbered (1-9) buffers. A preceding count is ignored. Put may be used in tandem with delete and yank operators to produce a flexible copy function.

Example

Put the contents of the named buffer a in the buffer above the current line.

    ''aP

QUIT

(1.6, 1.7)

Name

q, Q—quit the editor (q), switch to ex mode (Q)

Syntax

:q<CR> or **Q**

Description

The **q** command tries to leave the editor and return to the user shell. If there are any unwritten changes, the editor will tell you and ignore the request. You may override this by typing the variant :q!<CR>, which tells the editor to abandon changes.

The Q command immediately switches from the visual mode to the ex editing mode and maintains the same relative position in the editing buffer. You may return to visual mode by typing :vi<CR>.

Example

:q<CR>—leaves the editor unless there are unwritten changes to the editing buffer.

QUOTE

(5.3)

Name

^V, \—quote the next special character to make it visible

Syntax

^V*m*

Description

The quoting mechanism allows you to put control characters and other special characters into the editing buffer. Normally they would have an effect but not be seen, like the backspace character (^H). The \ quotes only the erase (^H) and line kill (@) characters (or whatever they are set to), while the more general ^V quotes all nonprinting characters.

Early versions of the editor used ^Q for this purpose. If the editor variable magic is cleared (nomagic), then all the special characters (called metacharacters), except ~ and $, lose their special meanings unless quoted with \.

Example

^V^L—quote the control-L character so it may be placed in the editing buffer as text instead of being interpreted as a command to redraw the screen.

READ

(7.2)

Name

:r—read a file or command output into the editing buffer

Syntax

:r file<CR> or **:r !cmd<CR>**

Description

The read command allows you to gather input from external sources (a file or command output) and place it in the editing buffer. The new material goes into the buffer as one or more new lines below the current line.

Example

Run the **date** command in a subshell and read it's output into the editing buffer below the current line.

:r !date<CR>

REDRAW

(6.5)

Name

^L, ^R—redraw or "refresh" the screen

Syntax

^L or ^R

Description

The redraw commands rewrite all or a portion of the screen to eliminate unwanted visual effects caused by noise, messages, and, on some terminals, @ symbols used to mark deleted lines.

The ^L command clears the screen and redraws it completely. ^R does not clear the screen and redraws only from the point of the first deleted line.

Example

Redraw the entire screen to remove a mail message.

^L

REPLACE

(4.3)

Name

r—replace the character at the cursor with another

Syntax

r*c*

Description

The single-character replace operator, **r**, replaces the character at the cursor position with the next character typed. The r operator is self-completing and needs no terminating **ESC**. This behavior is frequently used to split long lines by replacing a space or tab in the interior portion of a line with a RETURN character.

Example

Replace the character at the cursor with the letter d.

rd

SEARCH

(2.4, 10.4)

Name

/, ?—search forward or backward in the buffer for text

Syntax

/str<CR> or *?str<CR>*

Description

The search operators locate the first (maybe the only) occurrence of *str* in the editing buffer and place the cursor at the beginning of the found text string. / searches in a forward direction and ? searches in a backward direction.

If the editor parameter wrapscan is set, the searches will wrap around the ends of the buffer; otherwise they halt at the end or beginning of the buffer. Search strings may be specified by using the editor's regular expression syntax.

Example

/find-me!<CR>—move to the beginning of the string "find-me!".

——— *SET EDITOR VARIABLES* ———

(8.1)

Name

set—set or change the values of editor variables

Syntax

:set [no]*VAR*

:set **VAR** = value

:set **VAR** = string

Description

Set is an ex command that lets you configure the editor to suit your needs and ways of operating within fairly wide limits. To see a complete list of options and their current settings type **:set all<CR>** while in the editor command mode. Set options take one of three forms: a Boolean (on or off) item, a number, or a text string. Boolean options are set on by using their names as set parameters and are set off by prefixing "no" to the parameter name (list, nolist). Text strings are composed of letters, numbers, and special characters.

Example

Turn the automatic indentation feature on.

`:set autoindent<CR>`

SHELL

(8.3)

Name

sh, !—run a user shell or command from within the editor

Syntax

:sh<CR>

:!cmd<CR>

Description

Rather than leave the editor and lose your place, you can escape to a subshell temporarily (!) or indefinitely (**sh**) to run other programs. When the programs terminate, or when you quit the subshell by typing **^D**, the previous editing context is restored. Be careful not to start up a set of separate v i sessions while working in subshells. This is an easy mistake to make and is considered to be antisocial behavior in a multiuser environment because it can adversely affect system performance.

Example

!**ls -l**<CR>—run a long directory listing, then resume editing.

SHIFT

(9.6)

Name

>>, <<—shift line(s) right or left by shiftwidth

Syntax

n>> or *n<<*

Description

The shift operators move lines right or left by one shiftwidth. The count, *n*, (the default is one) specifies how many lines to shift.

Variations include the use of objects such as **G** (end of buffer) and */str* (to line containing str). The distance shifted is determined by the editor parameter **shiftwidth**, which you can control with the set command.

Example

Shift the current line and the following five lines to the right by one shiftwidth.

6>>

SHOWMATCH

Name

%—show matching parenthesis, brace, or bracket (showmatch)

Syntax

%

Description

The showmatch operator moves the cursor, which must be on a parenthesis, brace, or bracket, to the companion of a matched set. If the editor variable **showmatch** is set and you type a closing parenthesis, brace, or bracket, the editor automatically jumps the cursor to the matching opening one if it exists and is visible on the screen. If a match does not exist, the editor beeps to warn you. This feature is particularly important to Lisp programmers. The **showmatch** variable is set initially if the **lisp** variable is set.

Example

%

STATUS

(9.1)

Name

^G, :file—display the status of the current editing buffer

Syntax

^G or :file<CR>

Description

Typing either of these commands produces a one-line status summary of the current editing buffer and associated disk file. The summary shows the file name, whether it has been modified (the editing buffer contents differ from those of the file on disk), and the position of the cursor in the editing buffer (line x of y). Also, the distance the cursor has travelled into the file is expressed as a percentage of the file.

The **file** command can also take a file name argument. Typing the **file** command with an argument renames the file associated with the editing buffer. The original file, if there was one, is not changed.

EXample

:file<CR>—report information about the current editing buffer contents and its associated file.

SUBSTITUTE

(4.3, 10.4)

Name

s—substitute new text for existing text

Syntax

*n*s*text*ESC

Description

The substitute operator lets you substitute one string of characters for another, even if they have differing lengths. The optional count, *n*, tells the editor how many charcaters to delete. The newly substituted text may be of any length and is terminated by an **ESC**. Typing s without a count causes a substitution for the single character at the cursor. A variant of s, S, is actually a synonym for **cc** and operates on whole lines.

Example

Substitute the words "A longer phrase" for the next five characters starting at the cursor.

5sA longer phraseESC

TAB

(5.2)

Name

^I, TAB—insert a tab character into the editing buffer

Syntax

^I or TAB

Description

A special **TAB** key may not be available on your terminal, but the ^I combination will work on any terminal. While the editor is in the text insert mode, ^I inserts a tab character that will have a visible effect on the formatting of the text when it is viewed on the screen and printed out.

The tab characters have no effect in command mode and elicit a beep from the editor.

Example

Insert a two-column header in the editing buffer. The columns are separated from each other by a tab.

icolumn 1^Icolumn 2ESC

TAGS

(11.3)

Name

tags—move editing context to the tagged item specified

Syntax

:ta tag<CR>

Description

Tags provides a convenient way to find the file and line of an item of importance, like a function name in a program file. A tags file must have been prepared previously by using ctags or by manual means. Typing the :tag command causes the editor to find the file containing the tag and to move the editing context to the line containing the tag.

If the file being edited when the tag command is issued has changes that have not been written, you will need to write them or abandon them before moving to the tagged item.

Example

Write the current file and move to the file containing the function clrline( ):

```
:w | ta clrline<CR>
```

TRANSPOSE

(9.5)

Name

xp or Xp—transpose out-of-order characters

Syntax

xp or **Xp**

Description

This is a combination of two operators. The command effectively swaps two characters. Both **x** and **X** are single-character delete operators and the **p** is a "put after" operator.

The **Xp** form of the command takes a little getting used to but can be readily undone. The effect of the **xp** command is not reversible with a single command.

Example

Xp—transpose two characters reversibly.

UNDO

(6.1)

Name

u, U—undo the effects of editing commands

Syntax

u or **U**

Description

There are two flavors of undo. The **u** command reverses the effect of the previous editing command even if the command had global effect. The **u** command may undo itself, thus allowing you to "toggle" between two versions of text to see which you like better. The **U** command reverses the effect of a series of commands that affect the line containing the cursor provided you have not moved off the line containing the changes you wish to retract. U cannot be undone.

Example

U—undo all changes made to the current line since the cursor was last moved onto the line.

VERSION

(10.4)

Name

ver—display the version and release number of the editor

Syntax

:ver<CR> or :ve<CR>

Description

The version command let's you know the version and release numbers of the editor. Knowing that, you can have a general idea of what features are available to you. However, many system administrators or programmers tinker with vi on systems where source is available, so the version of vi/ex on your system may have been customized.

Example

:ve<CR>—display the editor's version and release number.

WRITE

Name

w—write some or all of the editing buffer to a file

Syntax

:n1,n2w *file*<CR>

Description

The write command has several variations. Without any parameters, **w** writes the entire editing buffer contents to the currently remembered file name, if any. Optional line numbers, absolute or relative, and a file name may be given to selectively write portions of the buffer to a file. The space between the **w** and *file* is mandatory.

Example

Create or update the file **newfile.txt** with the contents of lines 20 through 34 from the current editing buffer.

```
20,34w newfile.txt<CR>
```

XOUT

(4.2)

Name

x, X—delete (or "xout") a character

Syntax

*n*x or *n*X

Description

Both **x** and **X** take an optional count, **n**, that multiplies their effects. The **x** operator deletes one or more characters from the cursor position and to the right, and closes up the space left by the deletion. The **X** operator deletes **n** characters (default = 1) to the left of, but not including the cursor position, and similarly closes up the space.

Example

6x—deletes the current character and the next five.

— YANK —

(4.4, 4.5)

Name

y—yank a copy of text from the editing buffer

Syntax

ynOBJ

Description

The yank operator copies text from the cursor to the specified or implied object into a temporary buffer. **Y** is shorthand for **y$** (yank a copy to end of line), and **yy** means to yank copies of whole lines. Named buffers may be used to copy or move text from one editing buffer to another. The unnamed delete buffer may be used for the same purpose, but only in the current editing buffer.

Example

y)—yank a copy of the text from the cursor position to the end of the current sentence.

ZERO THE SCREEN

(3.7)

Name

z—"zero" the screen (size, position, cursor placement)

Syntax

nzm<CR> or *nzm.* or *nzm-*

Description

The "zero" operator adjusts the editing position in the file, the size of the viewing window, and the location of the cursor in that window. The value of *n*, if given, is the line around which the widow is adjusted. The optional *m* value specifies a window size in lines. The current size is used if none is given.

There are three possible command terminators: <CR> sets the current line, and, therefore, the cursor to the top line in the resulting window; dot (.) places the current line in the middle of the window; and a dash (-) places it at the bottom.

Example

10z8.—place line ten in the middle of an eight-line display window.

GLOSSARY

alternate file   The name of a file that once was current but was replaced when another file was made current. It may also be one that has been mentioned (such as when a **:read** command is invoked), but which has not yet become the current file. The alternate file is also known by the shorthand notation #.

argument list   A list of file names that can be given to the editor from the UNIX command line and from the **ex** command line within the editor.

buffer   A temporary storage area in memory or on a disk storage device. The vi/ex editor maintains as many as two editing buffers, and many temporary buffers named (a-z), numbered (1-9), and unnamed buffers.

character   A character is one of a set of symbols; most are visible (letters, numbers, punctuation marks), and some are not (control characters, special format codes).

crash   The result of some error or condition that causes a computer system to fail, usually in a catastrophic way. A crash may be hardware or software related.

current file   The name of the file currently being edited. When used as a file name, % is expanded to the name of the current file as it was specified to the editor originally.

cursor   A special marker, usually a blinking underline or block, that points to a character indicating the current position in the editing buffer.

escape   A mechanism for turning off (or on) the special meaning of a character. The editor uses the backslash key (\) to escape the special meanings of the character-erase and line-kill characters. Also, the escape key (**ESC**) that is used to terminate text insertion mode and some commands.

filter   A program that reads from its standard input and writes to its standard output. UNIX has many filter programs like grep, sed, sort, uniq, and others that may be "pipelined" to create a wide range of processing tools.

macro A simple character sequence (usually a single keystroke) that stands for something more complex. Macros provide a convenient shorthand notation for repetitive tasks.

mark A place holder in the editing buffer, analogous to a bookmark. Marks may be used to specify text objects for editing commands.

message line vi uses the last line of the screen to give you helpful information about the editing session (see also status line).

metacharacter A character that can have a special meaning in addition to its usual text meaning. *, ., \<, \>, $, and ↑ are just a few of the metacharacters you can employ while using the editor.

mode One of several states or conditions of the editor. Each mode has its own operating characteristics.

named buffer A temporary storage area for blocks of text. Each buffer is named by a letter of the alphabet.

numbered buffer A temporary storage area for blocks of text. Each buffer is associated with a number in the range from one to nine.

object Text items that have special significance to vi, such as characters, words, sentences, paragraphs, and sections, as well as screen positions, marks, and other items.

operator A word (or abbreviation) that tells vi what task to perform on default or specified objects.

overtype New text replaces existing text. As each character is entered, it replaces the one at the cursor position, and the cursor moves to the right one character.

parameter A value associated with a command. The parameter may cause a modification of a basic action of the command, or it may be used to return a result produced by the command.

pathname A UNIX word for a file or directory name preceded by a sequential listing of the directories leading to it. A pathname may be full or relative. A full pathname starts at root (/) and ends with the name of a file or directory. (Ex: /usr/ myname/myfile.) A relative pathname uses the current directory as a starting point. (Ex: ../other.)

pipeline A sequence of programs strung together with the UNIX pipe symbol (|). Except for the first and last programs in the pipeline, the output of each program becomes the input to the next program in the pipeline.

quoting Altering the special meaning of certain characters by using a preceding special symbol or command (\ and ^V). The backslash is used to quote or escape the line-kill and character-erase characters, and ^V provides a general quoting mechanism.

regular expression A string of characters, which may be a combination of normal characters and metacharacters, that potentially match a set of character strings. Regular expressions are used to specify line addresses and pattern matches for text substitutions.

relative pathname The pathname of a file stated in terms of the current directory as a starting point (../text/file).

status line The vi editor uses the last line of the screen as a status (and message) line. The editor also uses this line for temporary line-editing-mode commands such as those used to read and write files.

shell A UNIX user interface program that is both a command interpreter and a programming language.

shiftwidth Similar to tabstop, this is a value used by vi's shift commands (the default is eight columns).

string A sequence of characters.

split-screen The use of seemingly independent portions of the display for performing separate tasks, such as viewing two separate files. vi does not have this feature although it maintains a text display window of adjustable size and a status/command window of one line.

tab The common name for a tabulation character. Horizontal and vertical tabs format text into convenient blocks.

tabstop a value retained by vi that defines the number of screen columns equivalent to one tab character (the UNIX default is eight columns).

tag An entry in a data base called a "tags" file that identifies a function and its location in a program source file or a keyword or section in a document file. The `ctags` program available on some UNIX systems automatically produces a tags file for C program source files.

toggle Alternate between two conditions (analogous to a push-button light switch that has push-ON/push-OFF behavior). The editor has a set of Boolean variables that may be toggled.

undo Reverse the effect of the previous action or sequence of actions.

window A rectangular portion of the screen in which you will edit text or issue commands. `vi` lets you control the initial size of the editing window.

Supported
Terminals

There are literally hundreds of different video display terminal types being used daily on UNIX systems. The burden this puts on a program like vi is a heavy one. However, the virtual terminal interface provided by special program libraries (curses) and terminal data bases (termcap or terminfo) on most UNIX systems alleviates most of the potential problems.

You may wonder whether your terminal can run vi effectively. One way to find out is to search the **/etc/termcap** file for likely terminal identifications that might be used for your terminal. This can be done with the grep program. Assume you have a TeleVideo 920 terminal. The command

grep 920 /etc/termcap

will display every line in the terminal data base file that contains the "920" designation. You might also search for "televideo" or the commonly used "tvi" substitute.

Actual terminal identification strings are typed using numerals and lowercase letters, but manufacturer names and acronyms may contain uppercase letters, so you may need to do searches for several variations of the terminal name or manufacturer to be safe. If you use vi to examine the /etc/termcap file, set the editor variable **ignorecase** to obtain "caseless" search capabilities. Then the search for "televideo" will find "Televideo", "televideo", and the correctly spelled "TeleVideo" versions of the name.

The following table is a relatively current list of the terminals that can run the vi editor if they are properly identified to the system via the TERM variable or an acceptable alternative. The terminal types listed are known to work on at least one UNIX system. However, some of the types listed may not be available on your system. Other terminal types can be made to work with v i if suitable termcap entries are created for them. Appendix C describes a procedure for doing this.

Some of the terminals listed in Table A-1 are printing terminals. Although such terminals cannot be used with the editor in visual mode, they are listed for completeness and for use by the open mode of the editor and by other programs that need to know the characteristics of attached terminals.

Table A-1. Terminals capable of running the ex/vi editor.

Identification to UNIX	Make & Model
1200, tn1200	Terminet 1200
1620, 450	Diablo 1620
1640	Diablo 1640
2621, 2621a, hp2621, hp2621a	Hewlett-Packard 2621
	Hewlett-Packard 2621 (45 key-
2621k45, hp2621k45, k45	board)
	Hewlett-Packard 2621 (with print-
2621p, hp2621p	er)
2626p, hp2626p	Hewlett-Packard 2626 (printer)
2640, hp2640a, 2640a	Hewlett-Packard 2640a
2640b, hp2640b, 2644a, hp2644a	Hewlett-Packard 264x series
300, tn300	Terminet 300
3045, dm3045	Datamedia 3045a
3101, ibm, ibm3101, i3101	IBM 3101, Model 10
33, tty33, tty	Teletype Model 37
4025, 4027, 4024,	
tek4025, tek4027, tek4024,	
4025cu, 4027cu	Tektronix 4024/4025/4027
43, tty43	Teletype Model 43
8001	ISC 8001
912b, tvi912b, 912c,	
920b, 920c, tvi	TeleVideo 912/920 (new)
a980	ADDS Consul 980
aa, annarbor	Ann Arbor

(Continued.)

(Table A-1. Continued.)

Identification to UNIX   Make & Model

aaa, ambas, ambassador	Ann Arbor Ambassador (48 lines)
aaa30	Ann Arbor Ambassador 30 (dest BS)
aaa48	Ann Arbor Ambassador 30 (dest BS)
aaadb	Ann Arbor Ambassador 48 (dest BS)
aaagl	Ann Arbor Ambassador 48
adm2	Lear Siegler ADM2
adm3, 3	Lear Siegler ADM3
adm31, 31	Lear Siegler ADM31
adm3a, 3a	Lear Siegler ADM3a
adm42, 42	Lear Siegler ADM42
adm5	Lear Siegler ADM5
aj830, aj832, aj	Anderson Jacobson
ampex, d80, dialogue, dialogue80	Ampex Dialogue 80
ansi	ANSI standard CRT
big2621	Hewlett-Packard 2621 (48 line)
c100, concept, concept100	HDS Concept 100
c1004p	HDS Concept 100 (4 pages)
c100rv, c100	HDS Concept (rev video)
c100rv4p	HDS Concept 100 (rev video, 4 pages)
c100rv4pna	HDS Concept 100 (no arrows)
c100rv4ppp	HDS Concept 100 (printer port)
cdc456, cdc456tst	Control Data Corp 456
cdi	CDI 1203
compucolor	CompucolorII
d132, datagraphix	Datagraphix 132a
datapoint, dp3, dp3360	Datapoint 3360
delta, dd5000	Delta Data 5000
dg, dg6053	Data General 6053
digilog, 333	Digilog 333
dm1520, 1520	Datamedia 1520
dm1521, 1521	Datamedia 1521
dm2500, datamedia2500, 2500	Datamedia 2500
dm3025	Datamedia 3025a
dt80, dmdt80, dm80	Datamedia dt80/1
dt80132, dmdt80132	Datamedia dt80/1 (132 col mode)
dw1	DECWriter I
dw2, dw3, dw4	DECWriter II

(Continued.)

(Table A-1. Continued.)

Identification to UNIX	Make & Model
ep40, ep4000	Execuport 4000
ep48, ep4080	Execuport 4080
exidy, exidy2500	Exidy Sorcerer as DM2500
fox	Perkin Elmer 1100
ft1024, sun	Forward Technology graphics controller
gt40	DEC GT40
gt42	DEC GT42
h1000	Hazeltine 1000
h1500	Hazeltine 1500
h1510	Hazeltine 1510
h1520	Hazeltine 1520
h1552	Hazeltine 1552
h1552rv	Hazeltine 1552 (rev video)
h19, h19b, heathkit, heath-19, z19, zenith	Heath/Zenith h19
h19A, heathA, h19A, heathkitA	Heathkit H19 (ANSI Mode)
h19bs	Heathkit H19 (keypad shifted)
h2000	Hazeltine 2000
hp, hp2645, 2645	Hewlett-Packard 264x series
hp2626, hp2626a, 2626, 2626a	Hewlett-Packard 2626
hp2648, hp2648a, 2648a, 2648 terminal	Hewlett-Packard 2648a graphics
i100, gt100, gt100a	General Terminal 100A (formerly Infoton 100)
intext	ISC-modified Owl 1200
jgl, ambas, ambassador	Ann Arbor Ambassador 48
mdl110	Cybernex MDL-110
microterm, act4	Microterm ACT IV
microterm5, act5	Microterm ACT V
mime, mime1, mime2, mimei, mimeii	Microterm Mime-series
mime3a	Mime1 emulating ADM3a
omron	Omron 8025AG
owl	Perkin Elmer 1200
pe550	Perkin Elmer 550
plasma	Plasma Panel
qume5, qume	Qume Sprint 5

(Continued.)

(Table A-1. Continued.)

Identification to UNIX   Make & Model

Identification to UNIX	Make & Model
regent	ADDS Regent series
regent100	ADDS Regent 100
regent20	ADDS Regent 20
regent25	ADDS Regent 25
regent40	ADDS Regent 40
regent60, regent200	ADDS Regent 60
regent60na	ADDS Regent 60 (no arrow keys)
sb1, superbee, superb	Beehive Super Bee
sb2, sb3	Fixed Super Bee
sexidy	Exidy (smart)
soroc	Soroc 120
swtp, ct82	Southwest Technical Products CT82
t1061, t10, teleray	Teleray 1061
t3700, teleray	Teleray 3700 (dumb)
t3800	Teleray 3800 series
tek, tek4012, 4012	Tektronix 4012
tek4013, 4013	Tektronix 4013
tek4014, 4014	Tektronix 4014
tek4014sm, 4014sm	Tektronix 4014 (small font)
tek4015, 4015	Tektronix 4015
tek4015sm, 4015sm	Tektronix 4015 (small font)
tek4023, 4023	Tektronix 4023
teletec, tec	Teletec Datascreen
terak	Terak (emulating Datamedia 1520)
ti, ti700, ti733, 735, ti735	TI Silent 700
ti745, 745, 743	TI Silent 745
tvi910, 910	TeleVideo 910
tvi912, 912, 920, tvi920	TeleVideo (old versions)
tvi925, 925	TeleVideo 925
tvi950, 950	TeleVideo 950
vi200	Visual 200 (with function keys)
vi200f, visual	Visual 200 (no function keys)
vi200ic	Visual 200 (insert char)
vi200rv	Visual 200 (reverse video)
vi200rvic	Visual 200 (rev video/insert char)
vt100, vt-100, pt100, pt-100	DEC VT100
vt100n	DEC VT100 (no init)

(Continued.)

(Table A-1. Continued.)

Identification to UNIX   Make & Model

Identification to UNIX	Make & Model
vt100s, vt-100s, pt100s, pt-100s	DEC VT100 (132 cols, 14 lines)
vt100w, vt-100w, pt100w, pt-100w	DEC VT100 (132 cols)
vt132	DEC VT132
vt50	DEC VT50
vt50h	DEC VT50h
vt52	DEC VT52
wyse, w100	Wyse WY-100
x1720	Xerox 1720
xitex	Xitex SCT-100
z29, h29	Heath/Zenith z29
zen30, z30	Zentec 30
zen40, z40	Zentec 40
zen50, z50, Cobra	Zentec 50

Customizing
the Editor

You can influence the behavior of the ex/vi editor in several ways. If you will be using the visual mode, you must tell the editor what terminal type you are using. Beyond that, you may instruct the editor to operate in ways that suit your personal needs and preferences.

The Login Environment

Lesson 1 describes the procedure for identifying your terminal to the UNIX system. Then programs like vi and others that are screen-oriented will know how to interact with it, both to interpret keyboard input correctly and to display information on the screen in a meaningful way.

The procedure for telling the system about your terminal can be done manually with a few simple commands. Or you can place the needed commands in your shell startup file (.**profile** for the Bourne shell, sh, and .**login** for csh). See Lesson 1 for the details.

The Editor Start-Up File

An editor start-up file named .**exrc** may be used to tailor the editor. The ex part of the name comes from the name of the editor. The **rc** part means "run commands" and is derived from a technique used in the starting procedures for UNIX systems which reads a set of commands from a file named rc and executes them each time the system is started.

You can create a start-up file in your own "home" directory. Editor commands in it are read each time the editor is started. Some newer versions of the editor even permit you to have start-up in your other directories as well. If a **.exrc** file is found in the current directory, its contents are used instead of those in the **.exrc** in the home directory.

Any of the variables in Table 8-1 may be used in **set** commands to configure editor. Also, **map** and **abbreviate** commands may be placed in the start-up file. Here is an example **.exrc** file.

Response to the command **cd $HOME; cat .exrc**:

```
                                                              SCREEN DATA
 set autoindent
 set wrapmargin=15
 set report=2
 map ^[E :!ls -l^M
 . . .
```

The commands in the file turn on automatic indentation during insert, set a point 15 characters in from the right edge of the screen line where lines will be "wrapped" (a rudimentary formatting feature), report on the status line about any changes to the editing buffer that affect more than two lines, and set up a function key mapping.

EXINIT Variable

To speed up access to the start-up information, recent versions of the editor will look for a UNIX environment variable named **EXINIT** before looking for a **.exrc** file. If the variable is found, the values it contains are used, thus saving time compared to finding and reading a large file from disk and searching for the needed data.

An **EXINIT** variable that does the job of the **.exrc** file just described looks like this for sh:

EXINIT = 'set ai wm=15 report=2 | map ^[E ls -l'

export EXINIT

The commands would be added to a **.profile** file for execution once per logon.

For csh the appropriate command is

setenv EXINIT 'set ai wm=15 report=2 | map ^[E ls -l'

to achieve the same result. Notice that some of the variables names have been abbreviated to keep the command lines to a reasonable length. This command would be added to a **.login** file.

APPENDIX C | Writing TERMCAP Entries

When the array of general purpose video terminals that UNIX systems must work with is surveyed, it is apparent that complexity and confusion abound. Efforts to promulgate video terminal standards over the past seven or eight years are having an effect on new terminal designs, but there are still hundreds of video terminal types that differ from each other in many ways.

Screen-Oriented Programs

The terminal-interface problem becomes painfully apparent when you try to develop programs that gather user information in a data-entry form or workscreen. A program that is menu driven is another good example, and full-screen text editors and word processors are probably the most commonly used types of screen-oriented programs.

Each of these program types needs to interact with the user's video terminal in ways not possible with older line printing terminals. When the number of terminal and console display device types reaches into the hundreds, program developers' terminal-interface problems can compound rapidly.

Virtual Terminal Interfaces

Several methods have been developed to deal with the wide range of video terminals on the market. The concept is to write all screen-oriented software for a virtual terminal, one that does not exist, but which has at least a primary set of the capabilities thought necessary or desirable for full-screen interactions. The interface then provides a means of mapping calls to these virtual capabilities to those of real terminals. A comparable mapping is used to handle keyboard input to a program from disparate terminal types.

For a video terminal to be useable with a virtual interface it should have, as a minimum, the ability to move the cursor to any displayable position on its screen, either by absolute or relative means. Other features, such as scroll, screen clear, line and character insert and delete, and special video attributes, are nice to have; but, if they are not present in a particular terminal, they are either simulated by the interface or simply ignored.

Curses and Termcap

Curses and termcap originated at the University of California at Berkeley as a way of generalizing the video terminal interface to vi, the visual mode of the ex editor. Essentially an interpreted terminal data base arrangement, curses and the termcap data base are used in Berkeley UNIX and are available in modified form on many AT&T UNIX systems. Curses is a library of routines that control the placement of text on the terminal screen by using a set of terminal capabilities defined in a data base. Most versions of curses also provide routines that interpret keyboard input (text, commands, special function keys, and so on.).

Only full-duplex, alphanumeric video terminals are dealt with. Bit-mapped display terminals that can emulate the basic alphanumeric types can be handled, too. At the time of this writing, there are no officially supported routines to handle graphics and color in a standard way.

The termcap data base uses a set of variable names and values to describe each supported terminal. Terminal capabilities are grouped into three categories: numeric, string, and Boolean. One numeric capability, **co**, specifies the width of a screen line in columns. In the string category is **cl**, which specifies the string of characters needed to clear the terminal's screen. A Boolean capability is **bs**, which, if present in a terminal's description, says it can backspace with ^H (and possibly some other key that emits the same combination). There are more than 70 capabilities known to the curses library routines. Each capability has a two letter name (mnemonic in many cases). See the **termcap** entry in Section 5 of the UNIX User's Manual (or the equivalent for your system) for a summary of the capability designations and their definitions.

Here is what a terminal description in the termcap file looks like. This one describes the Lear Siegler ADM3a terminal. The first line is used to identify the entry. The colon-separated entries on the following lines constitute the description.

```
l a|adm3a|3a|l s i  adm3a:\
    :am:bs:cm=\E=%+ %+ :c l =^Z:co#80:\
    ho=^^:l i #24:nd=^L:up=^K:
```

This brief entry tells routines in the curses library that an ADM3a has automatic margins, can backspace using ^H, addresses the cursor with an "ESC=" sequence, clears the screen with a ^Z, and puts the cursor in the home position (upper left) with ^ (Ctrl-caret). It also defines an 80-column by 24-line screen and shows that ^L is a nondestructive space and ^K moves the cursor up a line (reverse linefeed).

None of the other termcap variables are listed because the ADM3a does not have those capabilities. If a program tries to highlight something on the screen by using what is termed "standout" mode, the request will be ignored because an ADM3a cannot display reverse video or any other character attribute that qualifies as highlighting the normal video attribute will be used.

An updated version of the curses library routines and a compiled terminal data base, terminfo, are officially supported on UNIX System V, Release 2. The newer library routines are faster and use the full insert and delete line and character features of terminals that have such capabilities. Older curses routines simulated the insert and delete effects in software.

The terminfo data base describes more terminals than the original termcap and is compiled for greater speed. Terminfo can use longer names for capabilities, so most have been renamed. A new data base entry format facilitates faster program startup and makes listings easier to read, too. In addition, terminfo expands significantly on the kinds of terminal capabilities that can be described and used in programs.

APPENDIX

D

Regular
Expressions

The term "regular expression" refers to text patterns that are used to match character strings. Regular expressions are widely used in the UNIX system. Pattern matching facilities are implemented as part of the shell (sh, csh, and ksh) and in numerous utility programs such as awk, grep, egrep, lex, and ed, and derivatives of ed, like sed, and the vi/ex editor. Various parts of this book have mentioned regular expressions and have given examples of their use. The material contained in this appendix is a description of regular expressions and additional examples of their application to editing tasks.

The primary metacharacters (characters that have been given special meaning) for specifying regular expression patterns are shown in Table D-1. There is an unfortunate lack of consistency among UNIX system programs in the precise definition of regular expression characters. Differences are noted in the table.

The table shows the characters that may be used to construct patterns to match text strings. All but the first (c) have special meanings when used in pattern specifications. Any character except the special characters listed in the table matches itself in a text string. Therefore, the search command **/baseball** given in the editor (vi, ex, ed) will match only the literal string baseball in the editing buffer. However, **/b.*ball** will match baseball, basketball, and beachball, as well as any other string that begins with "b" and ends with "ball" and that is not split across lines. The . matches any single character, and the * matches zero or more repetitions of whatever the preceding . matches, so . * matches any string of characters, including none.

Table D-1. Regular Expressions.

The first set of expressions are understood by all programs that provide pattern matching.

Expression	Description
c	Any single character that has no special meaning matches itself.
\c	A backslash turns off the special meaning of c.
. (dot)	Matches any single character. (NOTE: The shell uses ? for this purpose and treats dot as an ordinary character.)
↑	Matches the initial segment of a line. (Some application programs use % for this purpose.)
$	Matches the final segment of a line.
[...]	Matches any single character in the character class specified by the string within the square brackets.
[↑...]	Matches if the character is not one of the characters in the class specified by the enclosed string. (Some application programs use ˜ instead of ↑ to negate the class.)
e*	Matches zero or more occurrences of the regular expression, e.
e+	Matches one or more occurrences of the regular expression, e.
e?	Matches zero or one occurrences of the regular expression, e.
e1e2	Matches the concatenation of the regular expressions e1 and e2.

(Continued.)

(Table D-1. Continued.)

In addition to the above, the programs awk, egrep, and lex understand the following forms of expressions:

---

e1 | e2	Matches either e1 or e2. (The regular expressions may also be separated by a new line in place of the vertical bar.)
(e)	Matches the regular expression enclosed within parentheses.

An expression followed by a **+** matches one or more occurrences of the expression. Therefore, **/xa+** matches "xa", "xaa", "xaaa", and so on, but it does not match "x" by itself (**/xa*** does). A **?** matches zero or one occurrences of the preceeding expression. Therefore, **/xa?** matches "x", "xa", and nothing else.

The **^** and **$** metacharacters match beginning and ending line segments, respectively. The effect of **^** is that of "anchoring" the pattern at the beginning of a line. For example, **/^apples** matches "apples" only where it occurs at the beginning of a line. If **^** is not the first character of the pattern, it has no special meaning. **/apples$** matches "apples" only where it occurs at the end of a line. If **$** is not the last character of a pattern, it is an ordinary character and matches itself.

Character classes may be used to restrict patterns to a set of possibilities. Thus, **/[bhs]it** matches bit, hit, and sit. The negation of the set of possibilities, **/[^bhs]it** may be employed to match all three-letter words that end in "it" and begin with any letter except the ones specified. Therefore, nit, fit, and lit would match the pattern, but not bit, hit, and sit. The **^** loses its special meaning (negation) if it is placed anywhere in the set except in the first position.

Within a character set, a range of characters may be indicated by a dash separating the lower and upper characters of the range, such as a-z to match a lowercase letter, or 0-9 to match any single digit. The dash loses its special meaning if placed at the beginning of a set, so **/[-xyz^]** would match a literal -, x, y, z, or **^**.

The remaining combinations of regular expressions apply to programs other than the editors and will not be covered here. They are shown in the table for the sake of completeness only.

Other Screen Editors for UNIX

Lest you get the impression that **vi** is the be all and end all of screen editing for the UNIX system, be advised that there are many other screen editors including several very popular ones. One of the deficiencies of **vi** is its dependence upon modes for each activity. This means that a given key may have several uses, and its action depends on what mode the editor is in at the time of the keypress.

For example, the letter **w** is simply a letter in the insert mode, a command to move right to the beginning of the next word in **vi** command mode, and a command to write the editing buffer to a file in the **ex** command mode. This can be confusing, especially when the editor doesn't clearly tell you what mode it's in. (Recent versions of **vi** display mode messages on the status line if the **showmode** variable is set.)

Nearly all of the other screen editors for UNIX are modeless or nearly so. They generally behave like standard typewriters, by putting what you type directly into the editing buffer. Commands are entered with special control sequences or function keys. Cursor positioning commands are input by using arrow keys if they are available or special control sequences otherwise. Microcomputer users who have used WordStar and other wordprocessing and text editing programs are familiar with this approach already.

The following material is a summary of three alternatives to **vi** that have gained substantial following in the UNIX user community. EMACS is particularly popular with programmers because of its extensive built-in programming facilities and overall flexibility. INed (pronounced INN-ED) is the editor supplied with IBM's PC/

205

IX in place of vi. The EDIX screen editor traces its beginnings to the IBM PC and MS-DOS and it is now available on AT&T 3B UNIX computers and on some other UNIX systems as part of the Professional Writer's Package, which also includes a text formatter, an indexer, and a spelling checker.

EMACS

Depending on what UNIX system you are working on, there may be a copy of this editor or a look-alike kicking around somewhere, although it will probably not be officially supported. The original EMACS editor was written at MIT's Lincoln Laboratories by Richard Stallman. Another version by Bernie Greenberg was written in MacLisp for use under the Multics operating system. A popular commercial editor that emulates the behavior of the original EMACS and that uses the same name was written by James Gosling. Another EMACS look-alike that has been used for many years on UNIX systems within AT&T was written in C by Warren Montgomery. Stallman has recently released a public domain version of EMACS called GNU EMACS. This is the first wave of his effort to bring out a "free" version of the UNIX system.

The editor is invoked as **emacs** on most systems, and it accepts a range of command options and file names as arguments. EMACS is noted for unparalleled extensibility obtained through a macro programming feature, and in most versions, a Lisp interpreter or compiler. Modeless operation, multiple windows and editing buffers, and the sophisticated macro and Lisp programming features combine to produce a very capable editor. The penalty users face is a difficult-to-learn interface. Commands have limited mnemonic value and are not grouped logically, thus making EMACS a tough editor to learn. Fortunately, EMACS is easily extended and modified, thus allowing users to effectively create their own editors if they have some time and reasonable programming skills.

Most versions I've looked at tend to have an arrogant feel about them (flip error messages, disjointed and jargony documentation). Montgomery's is the exception. It is the most civilized regarding its interactions with users.

All versions have block move and copy functions, full regular expression search capabilities, and a host of editing convenience features. An unusual incremental search feature prompts for a search string and as each character is typed, the editor moves to the place in the file where a match is found, if any, to make it easy to know when enough characters have been typed to uniquely specify the text object being sought. The search may be combined with various forms of the replace feature to do global, local, and query-replace types of actions.

An on-line help feature called "apropos" is unique among screen editors for UNIX. It lets you type a key word and gives you a summary of relevant command information about that topic. For example, if you request information about the key word "buffer", EMACS would list all the commands that deal with buffers. You can then get detailed information about a particular command you want to use. Another help feature is a list of all terminal keys and their bindings. EMACS relates keys to actions by binding each key to a named macro or a procedure. Using this feature, you can customize EMACS for your own purposes. There are even tables of bindings that let EMACS emulate a vi-like editor for those who are have trouble breaking the vi habit.

Lisp programming support varies among EMACS versions. The Gosling version has MLisp (Mock Lisp), a Lisp-like interpreter that at least emulates Lisp syntax (love those parentheses!). It provides integer and string constants, names, and procedure calls. It has no **cons** function. Recent versions of Montgomery's EMACS use a precompiler (ECOMP) that accepts Lisp-like source to produce macro language procedures. The macro facility of this EMACS is admittedly a bit awkward and hard to program. The precompiler makes extending the editor a lot more pleasant task than it used to be.

You may configure EMACS automatically by using a startup file of EMACS commands or macro library functions (start-up files have names like .emacs__init and emacsini.ml). Using the various programming tools provided, you can make the editor be your own personal statement to the world about how editing should be done.

Like many things that are good for you, it is worth the effort to overcome the reaction to an unfamiliar taste or to the initial difficulties of a task for long-term gain. Experienced vi users in particular have difficulty adjusting to EMACS at first, but it's worth a try.

INed

The INed screen editor is the only visual editor available with IBM versions of the UNIX operating systems produced by Interactive Systems, spanning the range from PC/IX to VM/IX. The following is a summary of some of the major INed features. The PC/IX version was used as a basis for this summary. Because PC/IX is sold as a single-user system, INed runs only on the console screen.

On-screen formatting is provided in the form of paragraph fill and optional right justification. INed also allows filtering of portions of the editing buffer through PC/IX and custom filter programs. Blocks of text, either rectangular areas defined by a "box-mark" command or arbitrary regions defined by a "text-mark" command, may be copied or moved within a single file and between files.

INed has the requisite search capabilities. You may search forward or backward for literal strings of text only. An optional replace command substitutes a typed string for the most recently found match to a search. A global search and replace is not built into INed, but it is available via an external PC/IX program, rpl. Unlike the INed search option, rpl permits global search and replace operations by using regular expression syntax (wildcard characters permitted) in the search string.

One of the unique features of INed is "structured" files. A record of changes to a file being edited is maintained in addition to the file itself. Built-in INed commands manage structured files, and PC/IX has additional commands designed to manipulate structured files from the user shell.

INed permits files to be edited in one or more windows on the screen. Each window is marked by a fine-line border with the default window being a 20 line by 78 column area. An on-screen ruler is visible on the top line of the screen, and a two-line status area occupies the last two lines. INed continually reports the current cursor position, editing mode, and file name in the status area.

Menu interfaces are in vogue, and for good reasons they are likely to be with us for a long time. INed has an unobtrusive menu system that simplifies interaction with the host PC/IX user shell and assists users with many operations available in the editor. There are menus for "system" and "local" actions; both are modifiable to suit special needs. An associated feature is the very extensive help system that provides meaningful, context-sensitive help.

If you invoke INed without naming a file to edit, it reads the file $HOME/.estate to restore the previous editing state. The previous actively edited file is automatically loaded in such a case, and editing continues at the point where the previous session was terminated.

The editor has almost "modeless" operation. Because of the way INed is implemented, it treats the enter key (carriage return) specially. Instead of terminating the current line and opening a new line, it simply moves the cursor to the beginning of the next line and will scroll a line if it must to keep the cursor visible on the screen. Special commands must be used to insert one or more blank lines in the editing buffer.

The default text mode is insert. Overtype mode can be selected for replacing existing text rather than pushing it rightward to make room for new material. Cursor positioning uses the arrow keys and other commands, many formed by using the **Alt** key in combination with others. One major shortcoming of INed is the lack of forward and backward by "word" commands.

The INed editor may be customized at a generic system level and independently by each user. The system-level configuration file, /etc/eprofile, and the $HOME/.eprofile for each INed user tell INed what to do in a variety of circumstances. These are structured files that contain various forms and pointers to directories and files that are used to do everything from setting colors for the display to delivering prepackaged forms and help messages.

The help and error messages are very civilized. They say "touch a key" rather than the brutal "hit a key" of vi and so many other programs. INed is helpful and gracious in another way, too. It has excellent backup and recovery features that make it easy to recover from system failures and self-inflicted disasters. The cost is a bit more storage on disk, up to twice the amount of a standard ASCII file, but in critical situations, the security obtained is worth it.

EDIX

Originally designed for use on the IBM PC family of computers, this excellent editor is now available on many AT&T 3B-series UNIX systems as a third-party option. The appearance and behavior of the editor under UNIX differs a bit from its DOS counterpart, but it is nearly identical in most respects. The following description is based on a PC/IX version for OEMs that I tested from a PC/AT console. EDIX for UNIX systems uses the curses/termcap virtual-terminal interface and can be run effectively on the same video terminals that vi can.

EDIX is a modeless editor that was designed for ease of use. Some capabilities were sacrificed to keep operation as simple and straightforward as possible. Up to four windows and up to 12 editing buffers may be used at one time in an editing session. Word oriented operations (left, right, and delete) are provided along with simple cursor positioning commands (screen page up and down, start and end of file, and local motions).

EDIX has optional features such as automatic indentation, right margin with wordwrap, color display support, and settable tabs. The editor has minimal formatting capabilities, essentially limited to the wordwrap feature and a block reformatting feature. Far more sophisticated formatting capabilities can be handled by in-line "dot" commands and the companion text formatter package called WORDIX. The combination of EDIX and WORDIX makes a versatile word processing system.

Block operations such as moving, deleting, and copying groups of lines are supported. The most recent version (4.0) permits the begin and end marks of a block to be defined to character positions. Earlier versions worked over whole lines only. An undo stack of up to 50 lines may be used to recover "lost" lines.

A full regular expression search facility is provided. It may be used alone or in concert with a global or prompted replace feature. The combined search and replace feature is called the "translate" feature. A replacement may be done locally only, globally, or may be skipped under user control. A separate option is used to set upper- and lowercase equivalence, so searches may be made case-less if you wish.

EDIX has a macro facility that uses name-definition pairs to specify EDIX actions and text operations. The macros may be called by name and may be mapped to individual keys. Using macros, you can completely redefine the keyboard if you wish, and you may package repetitive and complex operations for invocation by simple keyboard commands.

Extended commands are available for interactions with the host operating system, including a "shell escape" that permits any built-in or external command to be run without leaving the editor. You may set configuration values from within the editor or from a configuration file that is read when the editor is invoked. A status display that reports salient information about windows, buffers, and files may be requested at any time. A cursor status report (column, row/max row) for the active window is not displayed by default, but may be activated and deactivated under user control.

EDIX has an on-line help system that delivers both general and context-dependent help information on request. Certain user and system errors automatically display messages. EDIX is accompanied by an excellent on-line "student" tutorial that is almost a substitute for the manual, but not quite. You should read the manual to pick up the fine points that are not described in the on-line tutorial.

An On-Line vi
Help System

The vi/ex editor has many commands and options—far too many to learn and remember even when you use the editor on a regular basis. Most users learn some minimal subset that lets them do the tasks immediately at hand. Then they may, from time to time, add new commands to their editing vocabularies as new situations demand.

——— *An On-line vi Help System* ———

What the vi editor lacks is an on-line help facility. Such a facility could be very helpful to beginning and experienced users alike. The following information describes an on-line vi help system that I designed to help my students use the vi editor effectively. It is a set of Bourne Shell programs and text files that deliver needed reminders and command summaries of up to a screenful in size for each of the primary editing commands and features that a user is likely to encounter.

All program source code is included in this book (Figures F-1 to F-4) so you can modify the system to suit your own purposes if they are not already met by the system. Shell scripts are used for greatest portability across UNIX systems. Some simple changes must be made to use the scripts under csh.

A template (Figure F-5) for the nroff text source files is included. The text of each manual page can be keyed in literally from the reference section of this book. You can easily create new or modified help frames by simply filling in the requested entries and processing the files with the programs provided.

If you wish to avoid the step of typing in all the program and text files, contact Omniware in Denver, Colorado at 303-368-7456 for information about how to obtain the system, ready to install and run on many UNIX-based systems.

———————— *System Description* ————————

The vi help system is based loosely on the "apropos" help system that is available on some UNIX systems of the Berkeley persuasion. A problem with the manual page orientation of the traditional UNIX documentation is that you have to know what you are looking for before you can find it—an electronic "catch 22." The program apropos, if available on your system, lets you request information by topic. It displays a summary of all commmands that are in some way related to the topic you specify using a data base of command names and descriptions created from the UNIX manual pages.

The vi help system does a similar job, but deals with the commands and functions of the vi editor exclusively. The system consists of several modules:

1. Text source files suitable for nroff processing. The source files should initially reside in the /usr/man/man.vi directory. The source files may later be archived to save space on the host machine. (Only the template is provided here, but the Omniware distribution contains all text files in source and formatted forms.)

2. Formatted manual pages for vi editing commands and features. The files reside in the /usr/man/cat.vi directory. If printed directly, they produce fully formatted manual pages. If accessed through the vi help commmand, **vihelp**, they are stripped of blank lines and presented as full or partial screens while retaining other page formatting features.

3. A data base of one-line help strings extracted from each of the manual pages. The data base file, **via.db**, resides in the /usr/lib directory.

4. Bourne Shell program files for administering the system. The files reside in the /etc directory and should be accessible only by the system administrator or someone with "superuser" authorization. The **mkhelp** program makes a help frame from a help text source file. The **mkvia** creates a new vi help data base file, **via.db**, from which information *apropos* to one or more specified topics may be obtained.

5. Bourne Shell files for general user accessing to the help information. These programs reside in the /usr/lbin or some other system directory that is accessible to all users. The **via** program takes optional arguments that specify topics of interest, and searches the vi help data base file for all entries that contain the argument strings, printing all lines that are matched. The **vihelp** program displays complete, but compressed, manual pages on the screen.

The help system has some limitations. It does not cover every command and feature of the editor. It has information about the most often used topics of vi, but no coverage of ex. Additional coverage can be easily added by using the tools provided to suit special needs and circumstances.

User's Guide

The manual pages that form the heart of the help system comprise the text of the reference section of *vi—The UNIX Screen Editor*. To aid you in finding needed detailed instructions and examples, each manual page refers to the relevant section(s) in the tutorial part of the book. If the section references do not provide adequate pointers to the information you need, use the book index.

Before you can use the vi help system you must set a shell variable to specify information needed by the some of the programs. the variable PAGER should be defined in your shell startup file (.profile or .login) to tell the help system programs what program your system uses to display information in chunks no larger than one screenful. Berkeley systems and others, like XENIX, that use Berkeley programs have more. The UNIX System V, Release 2 has a similar program called pg. Other systems may have a version of the print program, pr, that has a paging feature built in. In the worst case, you may have to specify cat and use the XON/XOFF contol functions (^Q/^S) **to start and stop the displaying of information on the screen.**

Select the command from the list below that works with your system and add it to you shell startup file:

PAGER=more

PAGER=pg

PAGER=''pr -t -p -l23''

(that's a lowercase "l", not a numeral 1 before the 23)

PAGER=cat

You must also add the line **export PAGER** to the file or add the variable name **PAGER** to an existing export list.

In addition, you must add the location of the **via** and **vihelp** commands to you PATH variable. By default this is /usr/lbin but you system administrator is free to put them in another directory. Assuming that /usr/lbin is used, add that name to you PATH in you .profile or .login shell startup file and be sure that PATH is properly exported (**export PATH**).

To get information about a vi editing topic while you are in the editor, type :**!via** *topic*<CR>. The program will display any lines in the vi help data base that pertain to the specified topic, scrolling the screen if necessary. The vi program will then prompt you to type a RETURN to continue editing.

Each line of the response shows the name of the manual page file that contains detailed information about *topic*, followed by a brief description of the editor command or feature. For example, if you type :**!via append**<CR>, the help system will deliver the line

append: a, A—append text to the editing buffer

Typing :**!via text**<CR> causes the system to display a set of lines, each of them containing a reference to **text**. To see all one-line help messages presented one screenful at a time, type :**!via**<CR>. You can also specify more than one topic on a single **via** command line to get a sequence of listings about topics of interest.

Use the **vihelp** command to get specific manual pages displayed. After using **via** to find out what command to use, you can use the command name that is the first component of the one-line message (e.g., **append**) to get a full manual page presented in compressed form on the screen. These manual pages are the same as those presented in the reference section of the book and are handy to have on line for those times when you do not have the book within reach. If you request more than one manual page, the pages are presented one at a time in the order requested.

To request a manual page while you are working within the vi editor, type **:!vihelp** *command***<CR>**. For example, to view the manual pages for "alternate file" and "buffer", type

> **:!vihelp alternate buffer<CR>**

As you can see by the example, the vihelp command expects you to know the name of the file that contains the manual page. This is the information you are given in the responses produced by the **via** command.

Administrator's Guide

The description early in this appendix gives you a view of the system's components and structure. The following is the detail you need to install and maintain the vi help system.

Two programs are used to maintain the vi help system. They should be placed in the /etc directory and made accessible only to authorized administrative personnel. The first, **mkhelp**, allows you to create new or modified manual pages. It takes one or more files in the /usr/man/man.vi directory and processes them to make displayable and printable manual pages in the directory /usr/man/cat.vi.

A source file called __form.n contains a template that can be used to create new source files. Copy it into a new appropriately named file and edit the new file. Then type **mkhelp** *filename***<CR>** to process the file. Do not type the **.n** extension. The program assumes a *filename***.n** in /usr/man/man.vi and creates a *filename***.vih** in /usr/man/cat.vi.

The program **mkvia** should be run after you have modified existing manual pages or created new ones. It keeps the vi help data base file up to date. The program's output is placed in the file **via.db** in the /usr/tmp directory. The file may require some editing and should be reviewed before putting it into service. When you are satisfied that it is ready for use, move it to the /usr/lib directory, which is where the **via** command expects to find it.

Users must have access to the programs **via** and **vihelp**, which should be placed in /usr/lbin or some other system directory that is accessible to all users. You should send mail to all users (or post a message in the "motd" file for some reasonable period) that instructs users what directory to add to their default PATH if the selected directory is one that they do not already access.

If you acquire a vi help system distribution from Omniware, it will usually include an installation program that will put everything where it belongs. It will also create needed directories if they do not already exist. But you may have to help users to get their logins set up correctly to use the system. See the user's guide section for details.

```
: mkhelp
#—set these directory names to suit your installation conventions—
SRC=/usr/man/man.vi
DEST=/usr/man/cat.vi
#—display a help frame if no arguments are specified—
if [ $# -eq Ø ]
then
   echo "Usage: $Ø fsrc..."
   echo "(Type fsrc without extension, e.g., append, not append.n)"
fi
#—loop through arguments, processing them one at a time—
while [ '%${1}%' != '%%' ]
do
   nroff -mm -Tlp -rN4 -rW72 ${SRC}/$1.n >${DEST}/$1.vih
   shift
done
```

Figure F-1. Program to format help frames from source files.

```
: mkvia
#—set these directory names to suit your installation conventions—
DEST=/usr/lib
SRC=/usr/man/cat.vi
TMP=/usr/tmp
#—create a null temporary database file—
# (overwrites an existing one)
echo >${TMP}/via.db
#—add a line for each command help frame—
for f in ${SRC}/*.vih
do
   #—get file name - trash the extention—
   fname=`basename $f | sed -e 's/\..*//'`
   #—get the one-line description, if any, from help file—
   desc=`grep ${fname} #{f} | # find lines containing the keyword sed
        -n 'l,ls/^//p'` # use first only; strip leading spaces
   #—append to the vi help database file—
   echo "${fname}: ${desc}">>${TMP}/via.db
done
#—display instructions for further processing—
echo "\nEdit the file ${TMP}/via.db\n"
echo"then move it to ${DEST}/via.db\n"
```

Figure F-2. Program to create the vi base "apropos" data base.

```
: via
# —name the vi help (apropos) database file—
DATABASE=/usr/lib/via.db
#—be sure a 'pager' program is set in shell environment —
# (use more, pr -t -l23 -p, or pg if available on your system)
if [ '%${PAGER}%' = '%%' ]
then
    PAGER=cat # not the best, but good enough
fi
#—process command-line arguments—
case $# in
Ø ) #—display the whole file and a help message—
   $PAGER $DATABASE
   echo '\nType '$Ø topic(s)' to limit output to specified topic(s).\n'
   ;;
1) #—display info about keyword entry—
   grep $1 $DATABASE | $PAGER
   ;;
*) #—loop through keywords one at a time—
   while [ '%${1}%' != '%%' ]
   do
      echo '$1:'
      grep $1 $DATABASE | $PAGER
      shift
   done
   ;;
esac
```

Figure F-3. Program to display one-line help messages.

```
: vihelp
CATFILES=/usr/man/cat.vi
#—process arguments-
case $# in
∅ )#—display a help message—
   echo 'Usage: $∅ name\07'
   ;;
*) #—display the help frame, stripping blank lines—
   cd $CATFILES
   while :
   do
      cat $1.vih | sed '/^[ ]*$/d'
      shift
      if [ '%${1}%' = '%%' ]
      then
      exit ∅
      fi
      echo '\nPress RETURN to continue... \c'
      read resp
   done
   ;;
esac
```

Figure F-4. Program to display help frames.

.ce
[title]
.sp
NAME
.in **+5**
[cmd—one-line description]
.in -5
SYNTAX
.sp
[syntax]
.in -5
.sp
DESCRIPTION
.in **+5**
[seven lines or less of description]
.in -5
.sp
EXAMPLE
.in **+5**
[brief example (1-2 lines)]
.in -5

Figure F-5. The manual page template for help frames.

INDEX

Related Resources Shelf

UNIX AND XENIX: A STEP-BY-STEP GUIDE
Douglas W. Topham and Hai Van Troung

Here's a truly unique guide designed for the first time users of the UNIX and XENIX operating system. Written for the 16-bit environment, this book covers UNIX commands, the C shell, the Visual Editor, text processing tolls, the Bourne Shell, and much more. Detailed appendices on vi options are also included.
1985/508 pp/paper/0-89303-918-7/$21.95

THE UNIX SYSTEM V SOFTWARE CATALOG
AT&T Technologies, Inc.

The new authorized reference manual of software products designed to run under the UNIX System V operating system. This comprehensive volume includes over 400 objective listings of UNIX software including information on Company Name, Product, Application Catagory, Product Description, Programming Language, Code Format, Hardware and Software Requirements, Supporting Computer Systems and Local Distributors.
1985/525 pp/paper/0-8359-8069-3/$19.95

ARTIFICIAL INTELLIGENCE FOR MICROCOMPUTERS: A GUIDE FOR BUSINESS DECISION MAKERS
Mickey Williamson

This book discussed the artificial intelligence from both an introductory point of view and a detailed look at expert systems and and how they can be used as a business decision making tool. Includes step by step instructions to create your own expert system and covers applications to cost/benefit analysis, and software benchtesting.
1985/300 pp/paper/0-89303-483-5/$15.95

To order, simply clip or photocopy this entire page, check off your selection, and complete the coupon below. Enclose a check or money order for the stated amount or include credit card information.
Mail to: Brady Computer Books, Dept. 3, 200 Old Tappan Road, Old Tappan, NJ 07675

Name _____

Address _____

City/State/Zip _____

Charge my credit card instead: MasterCard _____ Visa _____

Credit Card Account # _____ Expiration Date _____

Signature _____

Dept. Y   0928-9B